Migration, Education and Socio-Economic Mobility

The primacy of education in development agendas is unquestioned. With the gradual acknowledgement of the potential benefits that migration can hold for development, the relationship between migration and education is a growing area of research. *Migration, Education and Socio-Economic Mobility* explores how the decisions people make in terms of both their migration choices and educational investments, mediated as they are by gender, class, caste and nationality, can potentially contribute to earning incomes, building social and symbolic capital, or reshaping gender relations, all elements contributing to the process of economic and social mobility.

Much of the existing literature examining the links between migration and education focuses either on the investment of migrant remittances in the education of their children back home or on 'brain drain' that refers to the migration of skilled workers from the developing to the developed world. Most of these discussions are firmly rooted in materialist arguments and while undeniably important, tend to underplay the social processes through which migration and education interact to shape people's lives, identities and status in society. Along with economic security, people also aspire to social mobility and status enhancement. The ideas presented in this book take a more varied and nuanced view of the relationship between education and migration.

This book was originally published as a special issue of *Compare: A Journal of Comparative and International Education*.

Nitya Rao is Senior Lecturer at the School of International Development at the University of East Anglia, UK. She has over 25 years experience as a field-level practitioner, trainer, researcher and teacher. She has worked extensively in the field of gendered land relations, and her book *Good Women do not Inherit Land: Politics of Land and Gender in India* was published in 2008. She has also been involved in researching, from a gender perspective, issues of livelihoods and economic growth, with a focus on migration, education, resource access and social identity.

Migration, Education and Socio-Economic Mobility

Edited by
Nitya Rao

Routledge
Taylor & Francis Group

LONDON AND NEW YORK

First published 2012
by Routledge
2 Park Square, Milton Park, Abingdon, Oxon, OX14 4RN

Simultaneously published in the USA and Canada
by Routledge
711 Third Avenue, New York, NY 10017

First issued in paperback 2017

Routledge is an imprint of the Taylor & Francis Group, an informa business

© 2012 British Association for International and Comparative Education

This book is a reproduction of *Compare: A Journal of Comparative and International Education*, volume 40/ issue 2. The Publisher requests to those authors who may be citing this book to state, also, the bibliographical details of the special issue on which the book was based.

All rights reserved. No part of this book may be reprinted or reproduced or utilised in any form or by any electronic, mechanical, or other means, now known or hereafter invented, including photocopying and recording, or in any information storage or retrieval system, without permission in writing from the publishers.

Trademark notice: Product or corporate names may be trademarks or registered trademarks, and are used only for identification and explanation without intent to infringe.

British Library Cataloguing in Publication Data
A catalogue record for this book is available from the British Library

Typeset in Times New Roman
by Taylor & Francis Books

Disclaimer
The publisher would like to make readers aware that the chapters in this book are referred to as articles as they had been in the special issue. The publisher accepts responsibility for any inconsistencies that may have arisen in the course of preparing this volume for print.

ISBN 13: 978-1-138-11120-2 (pbk)
ISBN 13: 978-0-415-69351-6 (hbk)

Contents

1. Migration, education and socio-economic mobility
   Nitya Rao — 1

2. Aspirations and self-hood: exploring the meaning of higher secondary education for girl college students in rural Bangladesh
   Nicoletta Del Franco — 11

3. Aspiring for distinction: gendered educational choices in an Indian village
   Nitya Rao — 31

4. 'It is hard to stay in England': itineraries, routes, and dead ends: an (im)mobility study of nurses who became carers
   Sondra Cuban — 49

5. To fairly tell: social mobility, life histories, and the anthropologist
   Véronique Benei — 63

6. Marginal returns: re-thinking mobility and educational benefit in contexts of chronic poverty
   Bryan Maddox — 77

7. Standardized individuality: cosmopolitanism and educational decision-making in an Atlantic Canadian rural community
   Michael J. Corbett — 87

8. Whose education? The inclusion of Gypsy/Travellers: continuing culture and tradition through the right to choose educational opportunities to support their social and economic mobility
   Christine O'Hanlon — 103

Index — 119

Migration, education and socio-economic mobility

The primacy of education in development agendas is unquestioned. With the gradual acknowledgement of the potential benefits that migration can hold for development, the relationship between migration and education is a growing area of research. The main purpose of this Special Issue is to explore how the decisions people make in terms of both their migration choices and educational investments, mediated as they are by gender, class, caste and nationality, can potentially contribute to earning incomes, building social and symbolic capital, or reshaping gender relations, all elements contributing to the process of economic and social mobility.

Much of the existing literature examining the links between migration and education focuses on two types of relationships: first, the investment of migrant remittances in the education of their children back home; and second, the perspective of 'brain drain' that refers to the migration of skilled workers from the developing to the developed world. While it is true that remittances sent home by migrants can play a key role in funding children's education, as documented in studies in the Philippines (Yang 2004), El Salvador (Edwards and Ureta 2003) and Nepal (Thieme and Wyss 2005), to name a few, the level of investment depends on the immediate needs of the household, local investment patterns as well as an assessment of the quality of education and the likely returns from an investment in education. The correlation need not always be positive and in some instances migration can actually create disincentives for education.

Similarly, while migration of the skilled or highly educated from developing countries is widely viewed as a problem for these countries, for the highly skilled migrants themselves, this often represents an opportunity to further their training and skills acquisition. In fact, some people may even move in order to improve their educational prospects, whether this involves attending university or acquiring professional qualifications abroad, or through moving from rural to urban areas to attend better-run schools, or take up apprenticeships in trades with growing demand. In either case, one needs to remember that the outcome is not fixed, as migration carries within it significant risks and costs – and may not always result in overt improvements in education for the migrants or their family members.

Both the inter-relationships between migration and education discussed above are firmly rooted in materialist arguments and while undeniably important, tend to underplay the social processes through which migration and education interact to shape people's lives, identities and status in society (Gardener and Osella 2003; Jeffrey, Jeffrey, and Jeffrey 2008). Along with economic security, people also aspire to social mobility and status enhancement. This Special Issue seeks to open up some of these areas for discussion, going beyond the conventional debates around remittance use and brain drain.

Pathways to mobility

The notion of mobility underlies much of the literature on poverty reduction and social change. With each successive generation, there is an aspiration to change the course of one's life and improve one's standard of living, though sometimes and particularly for the poor, this involves a struggle to just maintain one's position in the face of natural disasters, economic crisis or social threats. People confront a range of constraints in their attempts to achieve upward mobility, some material, but many social and ideological, for instance, caste hierarchies in India or gender norms and race relations globally, that serve to legitimise particular interests, power relations and divisions of work, and justify social difference. People's experiences of mobility can then be understood as attempts to change the relational dynamics of social domination with a view to achieving a greater measure of equality for themselves and their families in society, both in terms of opportunity and life chances (Young 1990; Piketty 1995; Blanden, Gregg, and Machin 2005; Erikson and Goldthorp 2002).

Change occurs not only from above, through legislation and policy measures that seek to address discrimination and promote equality, but equally from below. There are many ways in which people try to change their lives: through diversifying livelihoods, through better education, through building social networks (social capital), through reducing present consumption for future accumulation, through constructing alternate narratives of their lives, through having more or fewer children, through moving. The strategies adopted ultimately depend on the resources available to a particular individual in terms of money, their own skills and capacities, their social support networks and household responsibilities, and social norms and expectations, as individuals are socially embedded and rarely are such decisions made in isolation (Curran 1996). Further, outcomes are not just context-specific, but are also contingent on larger state policies and market responses in relation to both education and employment (Hashim 2005; Rao 2009; Skeldon 2006; Thorsen 2005). Despite the constraints, as Bertaux and Thompson note, a sufficient number respond to opportunities provided by the 'local and national economy, access to education, means of travel and social imagination' (1997: 2).

Migration has been a key channel for mobility – an opportunity to earn money, see a new place, experience new cultures, gain skills and accumulate consumption goods. In the case of overseas migration, particularly to the Gulf countries, for instance, one finds that much of this is unskilled or semi-skilled and relatively low paid, yet the difficulties are far surpassed by the very experience of travel to a distant land and the bringing back of gifts and the status and prestige this entails (Siddiqui 2003; Pahl and Rowsell 2006). Migration however is a varied process, it can be seasonal and short term, or for a much longer duration, even permanent; it carries varying levels of risk in terms of security, payment of wages and legality and consequently has differential implications for earnings, remittances and consumption; it requires different levels of skills and resources, both financial and social.

There is a need to distinguish between these different types of migration: internal and external, migration that is voluntary (even though driven by economic need) or forced (under conditions or war or conflict), as the variation in the circumstances of migration does result in differential needs and strategies, especially in relation to educational investments. Most of the papers in this issue deal with voluntary migration, yet it is important to clarify the conditions under which migration is undertaken and the nature of the process as this mediates final outcomes, whether in terms of responding to immediate survival needs or aspirations for accumulation of both material and symbolic wealth. The decision to migrate then is a complex one, involving a range of trade-offs in terms of allocation of household funds, sale of assets, child work (and/or withdrawal from school) or investment in further education (Kothari 2002).

Schooling and formal education has been seen as another major route to socio-economic mobility – the path to secure skilled and better paid jobs, but more importantly, for its role in the expansion of opportunities for individuals in society and as a catalyst for social change (Dreze and Sen 1995, 109). Democratisation is expected to ensure equitable access to basic education for children of all social categories, especially in the context of Education for All (Dyer and Rose 2005). While this does contribute to a higher level of awareness about modern institutions and in turn an ability to protect oneself from exploitation, and a level of self-worth, self-confidence and social prestige, it does not necessarily lead to improved employment opportunities, and as Jeffery, Jeffery, and Jeffery (2008) demonstrate in their study in North India, money, power and social networks appear to be more important for accessing jobs than educational credentials. In fact, unemployment may even increase with better educational levels as the educated are more discerning about the kind of job they engage with and the respect attached to it, aspiring to more prestigious white-collar work and rejecting manual labour. Migration sometimes offers a way out of this employment impasse for the educated, enabling them to undertake lower-status jobs at a distance from their locality and community, in the anonymity of an urban metropolis perhaps. They compensate for this loss of prestige at the workplace through enhanced consumption in their homes and personal lives, giving an appearance of wealth, leisure and in turn status (Rao 2009).

The policy emphasis on schooling has, however, further devalued the role of informal learning, whether through social networks or in relation to migration and the exposure to new cultures. Schooling has now become the prerequisite for occupational ambition, with even poor parents often willing to sacrifice immediate consumption and personal expenses to send their children to fee-paying private schools (Caddell and Day Ashley 2006; Rose 2009). Yet schooling is also seen to reproduce social and economic inequalities and hierarchies by justifying privilege and attributing poverty to personal failure. Children from working-class families consistently underachieve at every level within the education system compared with middle- and upper-class children, explained by Bourdieu in terms of 'class habitus' or the distinctive cultural and knowledge systems that enable the upper classes to relate more easily to what happens in school (Bourdieu and Passeron 1977).

In the current context of globalisation and widespread migration, outcomes, nevertheless, can be different, with educational encounters having 'both reproductive and transformative potentials' (Collins 2009: 1). While maintaining class, race and gender divisions in the labour market, returns from migration, especially across borders, are often higher, enabling status shifts in the local context. Further, the experiences and outcomes of schooling can be different for boys and girls. While gender is often not an explicit focus of either migration (DRC 2009) or education research (Arnot and Fennell 2008), educational aspirations, migration experiences and well-being outcomes are all gendered, and in contexts such as South Asia, establishing particular sets of gender relations remain central to the process of social mobility.

In terms of the links between migration, education and mobility then, as mentioned in the introduction, the major global debate has centred around skill transfers and brain drain versus brain gain. In fact, there has been a call by developing countries to be 'paid' for the 'professional exodus', as reflected for instance in the Commonwealth Protocol for Recruitment of Teachers (Commonwealth Secretariat 2004; Morgan et al. 2006). A second issue has been the investment of migrant remittances in education. One finds a lot of variability in remittance use patterns to establish any form of causality between migration and educational improvements (Siddiqui and Abrar 2002; Ozden and Schiff 2006). McKenzie and Rapoport's (2007) study of Mexican migrants found that educational achievements were in fact lower in migrant as compared to non-migrant households since the jobs in the USA were comparatively high-paying but low-skilled, hence would not be attractive to educated youth. Further social networks here seemed to play a more crucial role than education. While important for securing employment, in particular for migrant workers, such networks, however, pose limits on individual mobility by creating a pressure for downward levelling, thus also contributing to the reproduction of social norms rather than their transformation.

Yet there need not always be a trade-off between the strength of social networks and educational investments. Robinson-Pant (2001), for instance, found that literacy facilitators in Nepal saw their involvement with non-governmental organisations and their education programme as an opportunity to become a part of new networks (the 'development' family), with possible access to new resources in the future. Munshi and Rosenzweig (2003) too point towards the new opportunities offered by education, including in terms of unconventional marriages, or new jobs not associated with particular castes or classes of people. Similar is the case with students migrating to institutions of higher education, with the formation of networks and connections with influential people and institutions driving the investment in education.

Methodological imperatives

Structural constraints remain, yet these are not insurmountable, and people exercise their agency in many different ways in order to do so. Social mobility research has tended to focus on inter-generational shifts in social standing as measured by educational achievements and their transition to occupational outcomes. As Bertaux and Thompson (1997) point out, this simplification is partly a result of the domination of this field of research by economists using the survey method, seeking generalisations rather than complexity and difference. Individuals are embedded in their families and local contexts, and influenced in their decisions also by market opportunities and state policies. Their interpretations as well as the representations of their experiences then equally form a part of their subjectivities and lived realities, since education–work transitions are not straightforward, especially in the case of migrants, whose work motivations might be quite distinct from that of local populations. Anthropological critiques have influenced more recent economic research in this field, which in accepting that wealth, race and schooling are all important for the transmission of economic status across generations (Bowles, Gintis, and Groves 2005), acknowledge the role played by individual subjectivities and social identities in the experience of mobility.

The papers in this collection primarily use a range of qualitative and ethnographic methods to explore the meanings and dimensions of mobility and its relationship with processes of migration and varied levels of educational attainment. These are located within a larger context shaped simultaneously by universal state policies and principles of non-discrimination with respect to education provision, and the persistence of strong social norms in relation to occupational and social differentiation. These methods are crucial for capturing the complexities inherent in processes of mobility that are at the same time contextual, contingent and contradictory.

Papers in this collection

While much of the debate in the mobility literature, drawing on its base in economics, relates to the returns from schooling, the papers in this collection present a more varied and nuanced view of the relationship between education and migration. Four of the papers directly address the issue of the links between formal educational credentials, migration and mobility (Benei, Cuban, Del Franco and Rao), while the remaining three question the primacy placed on schooling in studies of mobility (Corbett, Maddox and O'Hanlon).

First, in thinking about the transformative role of formal schooling, Del Franco shows how higher education for Bangladeshi girls contributes to the development of their sense of selfhood, and personal agency, and unlike their younger counterparts, who stop studying in order to get married, girls who enroll at college develop more complex and differentiated aspirations for the future. By prolonging in temporal terms their transition to adulthood, these girls find the formal educational system quite empowering in their personal lives, even though the ultimate outcome might be marriage rather than an independent career or working life.

Rao, in her paper, points to the somewhat contradictory effects of formal education for a marginalised, ethnic minority group (Scheduled Tribe) in eastern India, emerging from the social identity of the students. Parents and young adults creatively invest in the choice of particular types of schooling that are socially valued, for the lifestyles and culture they inculcate. Private schools, in this case mission-run schools, are seen as contributing to the development of personal characteristics including dress, speech and deportment that can lead to enhanced social status and prestige, and are hence preferred. These attributes can also contribute to manipulating existing social hierarchies and accessing new networks and opportunities. Despite such investments, outcomes however are often constrained by the nature and segmentation of migrant labour markets, with ethnicity here serving to exclude them from both white-collar employment and private enterprise, despite acquisition of formal education.

Cuban illustrates this point in the case of international migration. She shows how skilled migrant nurses from South Asia to the UK are ideologically and socially represented as 'deskilled' care-workers, performing an important job, yet one that is low paid (in the context of the destination) and socially devalued. While the nurses use a range of strategies to advance their careers, from choosing reputed hospitals for training in their home countries, attending and taking English-language tests etc., many of them fail to overcome the structural barriers that stop them becoming full-fledged health professionals in a new country.

The relationship between determinism in terms of mobility outcomes and contingency in the everyday lives of people is brought out clearly in Benei's paper. Focusing on a single formerly 'untouchable' family, she finds evidence of spatial mobility leading on to considerable gains in both economic and educational terms, as reflected in the everyday lifestyles and consumption patterns of the family under study. Yet it was in the social realm that they found it more difficult to erase the mark of untouchability and the stigma associated with it. Hence despite conducting themselves as ordinary middle-class citizens, there remained an ambiguity in terms of their social standing, which made their account of mobility much more complex than standard survey data could have revealed.

The remaining papers question the assumption that the links between formal schooling, migration and mobility are necessarily positive. Maddox argues for the need to rethink this conceptualisation in contexts of chronic poverty, where many people have access only to poor-quality schooling or no schooling at all. When people experience multiple constraints and vulnerabilities, educational returns may be experienced as small incremental benefits, what he terms as 'marginal returns', rather than any significant increase in incomes. Poor women in particular move between the pressures of survival and the aspirations for stability and growth in their choice of activities, often leading them to adopt low-risk, low-return strategies rather than going for growth through risky educational investments.

Corbett, discussing youth aspirations in an Atlantic Canadian rural community, points to the importance of place and space in understanding local educational choices. Using examples of formal and parallel graduation celebrations, he points to the tensions between the local, place-based culture that demonstrates traditions of local conjugal reproduction and the habitus of adult work in the community, and the mobility imperative embedded in formal schooling, which reflects ideas of individuality and consumerism much more than collective cultures. He also points to how inequality is reproduced through the schooling process, with only those youth with time, space and identity being able to satisfy the requirements of formal schooling.

O'Hanlon further emphasises the theme of reproduction of social inequalities in the context of Gypsy/Traveller communities in the UK. State policy seeks to extend education provision to these communities, seeing them as lying on the margins of mainstream society, and needing to be 'included' in the mainstream, without recognising the specificities of and needs deriving from their lifestyles, skills and traditional knowledge. She uses the Freirean concepts of conscientisation and politicisation to argue that rather than being assimilated into mainstream society, often as failures, due to low-quality provision, poor health and living conditions, incompatibility of schooling with migrant lifestyles and language difficulties, educational provision should enable the travellers to find an effective language for communication and empowerment, thus making a plea for a broader understanding of education.

Clearly, while formal education does have a role to play in facilitating mobility, both social and economic, the relationship is by no means straightforward, especially in the context of migration, which could involve exposure to new forms of certification, new skills, new cultures and new standards of measurement. It can lead to downward mobility as in the case of the migrant nurses to the UK (Cuban), or further marginalisation as in the case of the travellers (O'Hanlon), but can also offer some opportunities for resistance and transformation, even though constrained by social norms and culture (Benei, Corbett, Rao and Del Franco). In some cases, people set up alternatives to the formal system, hoping to secure their livelihoods and attain a degree of mobility by shifting the very terms of the discourse as illustrated by the non-schooled adults in Bangladesh (Maddox). Clearly all the experiences have some positive and some negative elements, but causality is hard to establish, as outcomes remain uncertain and contingent on particular time-space conjunctions.

Future directions

The major conceptual contribution of this Special Issue of *Compare* is then in trying to locate the relationship of education to social and economic mobility in a context of migration. Education contributes to migration directly through responding to the demand for particular skill sets in labour markets at the destination. While these are recognised as valuable skills, they are often devalued, not because of the quality of skills *per se*, rather due to the identity of the persons carrying those skills. Education is then not an independent variable, but its value is influenced and shaped by the social context and social identity of the bearer of the skills, distinguished by gender, but equally by race, caste and ethnicity.

In the other direction, migration is seen to contribute to educational provision and attainment in at least two ways: first, by using remittance money for sending children to school, and second, by creating a demand for particular sets of skills and thus encouraging people in sending areas to invest in acquiring those skills. But here again the evidence is mixed. Confronted by a process of deskilling at the destination, many migrants prefer not to put their children through several years of schooling. Rather, they invest in vocational skills acquired through apprenticeship or other forms of non-formal or informal learning, in strengthening social networks though marriage and dowry transactions or then in productive assets such as land or consumption expenditure that can enhance their social standing within the community and thereby open up new channels for information, communication and mobility.

The papers in this issue have attempted to give voice to present and potential migrants, young men and women continuing in formal education and those outside it, to gain an understanding of their own perspectives on their educational experience and its contribution to future mobility. This is a small beginning in the direction of understanding the motivations and subjectivities of parents, children and youth in terms of the choices and decisions they make in relation to both education and migrant employment. More research is needed in this field, particularly to gain the perspectives of children who end up moving with their parents, often not out of choice (as in conflict or crisis situations), denied both stability of residence and opportunities for learning during their childhood. Policy responses to deal with the education of mobile populations too need further thought.

References

Arnot, M., and S. Fennell. 2008. Gendered education and national development: Critical perspectives and new research. *Compare* 38: 515–23.
Bertaux, D., and P. Thompson. 1997. *Pathways to social class: A qualitative approach to social mobility*. Oxford: Clarendon Press.
Blanden, J., P. Gregg, and S. Machin. 2005. *Intergenerational mobility in Europe and North America*. London: Sutton Trust.
Bourdieu, P., and J.-C. Passeron. 1977. *Reproduction in education, society and culture*. London and Beverly Hills, CA: Sage.
Bowles, S., H. Gintis, and M.O. Groves, eds. 2005. *Unequal chances: Family background and economic success*. New York and Princeton, NJ: Russell Sage Foundation and Princeton University Press.
Caddell, M., and L. Day Ashley. 2006. Blurring boundaries: Towards a reconceptualisation of the private sector in education. *Compare* 36: 411–9.
Collins, J. 2009. Literacy as social reproduction and social transformation: The challenge of diasporic communities in the contemporary period. Plenary presentation at the International Conference on Literacy Inequalities, September 1–3, in Norwich, UK.

Commonwealth Secretariat. 2004. *Commonwealth teacher recruitment protocol.* London: Commonwealth Secretariat.
Curran, S.R. 1996. Intra-household exchange relations: Explanations for gender differentials in education and migration outcomes in Thailand. Working Paper Series 96–12, Center for Studies in Demography and Ecology and Battelle Population Research Group, University of Washington, Seattle.
Development Research Centre (DRC). 2009. *Making migration work for development.* Brighton: Development Research Centre on Migration, Globalisation and Poverty.
Dreze, J., and A. Sen. 1995. *India: Economic development and social opportunity.* New Delhi: Oxford University Press.
Dyer, C., and P. Rose. 2005. Decentralisation for educational development? An editorial introduction. *Compare* 35: 105–13.
Edwards, A.C., and M. Ureta. 2003. International migration, remittances, and schooling: Evidence from El Salvador. *Journal of Development Economics* 72: 429–61.
Erikson, R., and J.H. Goldthorp. 2002. Intergenerational inequality: A sociological perspective. *Journal of Economic Perspectives* 16, no. 3: 31–44.
Gardener, K., and F. Osella. 2003. Migration, modernity and social transformation in South Asia: An overview. *Contributions to Indian Sociology* 37, nos. 1–2: v–xxviii.
Hashim, I.M. 2005. Exploring the linkages between children's independent migration and education: Evidence from Ghana. Migration DRC, Brighton. www.migrationdrc.org/publications/working_papers/WP-T12.pdf.
Jeffrey, C., P. Jeffery, and R. Jeffery. 2008. *Degrees without freedom? Education, masculinities and unemployment in North India.* Stanford, CA: Stanford University Press.
Kothari, U. 2002. Migration and chronic poverty. Working Paper No. 16, Chronic Poverty Research Centre, Institute for Development Policy and Management, Manchester.
McKenzie, D., and H. Rapoport. 2007. Network effects and the dynamics of migration and inequality: Theory and evidence from Mexico. *Journal of Development Economics* 84, no. 1: 1–24.
Morgan, J., A. Sives, S. Appleton, and R. Bremmer. 2006. Teacher migration from Jamaica: Assessing the short term impact. *Caribbean Journal of Education* 27, no. 1: 85–111.
Munshi, K., and M. Rosenzweig. 2003. *Traditional institutions meet the modern world: Caste, gender and schooling choice in a globalising economy.* Cambridge, MA: Massachusetts Institute of Technology, Department of Economics.
Ozden, C., and M. Schiff, eds. 2006. *International migration, remittances and the brain drain.* New York: Palgrave Macmillan.
Pahl, K., and J. Rowsell, eds. 2006. *Travel notes from the new literacy studies: Instances of practice.* Clevedon, UK: Multilingual Matters.
Piketty, T. 1995. Social mobility and redistributive politics. *Quarterly Journal of Economics* 110: 551–84.
Rao, N. 2009. Gender differences in migration opportunities, educational choices and wellbeing outcomes. Migration DRC, Brighton. www.migrationdrc.org/publications/research_reports/finalreportJan2009nitya[1]MWFeb26.pdf.
Robinson-Pant, A. 2001. *Why eat green cucumber at the time of dying? Exploring the link between women's literacy and development: A Nepal perspective.* Hamburg: UNESCO Institute for Education.
Rose, P. 2009. Editorial introduction: Non-state provision of education – evidence from Africa and Asia. *Compare* 39: 127–34.
Siddiqui, T. 2003. Migration as a livelihood strategy of the poor: The Bangladesh case. Paper presented at the Regional Conference on Migration, Development and Pro-poor Policy Choices in Asia, June 22–24, in Dhaka.
Siddiqui, T., and C.R. Abrar. 2002. *Contribution of returnees: an analytical survey of postreturn experience.* Dhaka: International Organisation for Migration (IOM) Regional Office for South Asia.
Skeldon, R. 2006. Globalization, skilled migration and poverty alleviation: Brain drains in context. Migration DRC, Brighton. www.migrationdrc.org/publications/working_papers/WP-T15.pdf.
Thieme, S., and S. Wyss. 2005. Migration patterns and remittance transfer in Nepal: A case study of Sainik basti in Western Nepal. *International Migration* 43, no. 5: 59–98.

Thorsen, D. 2005. *Looking for money while building skills and knowledge: Children autonomous migration to rural towns and urban centres [A field report from Burkina Faso].* Migration DRC, Brighton. www.migrationdrc.org/publications/research_reports/DorteFieldReport2005_English.pdf.

Yang, D. 2004. *International migration, human capital, and entrepreneurship: Evidence from Philippine migrants' exchange rate shocks.* Ann Arbor: University of Michigan Press.

Young, I. 1990. *Justice and the politics of difference.* Princeton, NJ: Princeton University Press.

Nitya Rao
University of East Anglia, UK

Aspirations and self-hood: exploring the meaning of higher secondary education for girl college students in rural Bangladesh

Nicoletta Del Franco

Institute of Development Studies at the University of Sussex, Brighton, UK

> This study focuses on girl college students in a rural area of South West Bangladesh exploring the meaning and value they give to higher secondary education. By listening to their voices, the ethnography shows that unlike their younger counterparts, who stop studying in order to get married, girls who enrol at college develop more complex and differentiated aspirations for the future. They show a strong sense of self-worth and self-esteem in articulating publicly their hopes of becoming economically independent and more in control of important life choices. The study suggests that, by prolonging in temporal terms the transition to adulthood, higher secondary education challenges girls' perception of themselves, favours the development of a different sense of self-hood. and increases their agency and capacity to negotiate their own ways of being part of their families and their society.

Beyond human development and empowerment: girls' education and self-hood

In this paper I focus on the experiences, expectations and aspirations of a group of girls going to Intermediate college[1] in a rural area of South West Bangladesh. By listening to their voices this study provides insights into the value and meaning girls give to their experiences as college students and into their motivations in pursuing higher secondary education, beyond the factors that motivate their parents' commitments to their studies. I discuss the extent to which education becomes for them a constitutive element of an emerging and contested phase of transition to adulthood and its profound implications for their sense of self-hood and self-esteem.

My analysis of the value and meaning of education for this group of young women is located in the context of what social anthropologists have termed the social embeddedness that characterizes most of South Asian rural society where individuals are bound into a complex web of social, hierarchical relationships (Kakar 1978; Jeffery and Jeffery 1996 ; Kabeer 2000; Ewing 1991). Broadly speaking this literature problematizes the extent to which social actors in these situations act as autonomous individuals. This issue has been taken up specifically in relation to women's agency, with a significant literature suggesting that women's capacity to act in accord with their perceived needs and to voice their concerns, in short to exercise agency, may be limited and shaped in particular ways (Raheja and Gold 1994; Jeffery and Jeffery 1994, 1996; Haynes and Prakash 1992, Mc Leod 1992; Kabeer 2000). A focus on agency is also apparent in research exploring young people's construction of social identity through ongoing processes of negotiation within complex social relations in studies of youth culture in South Asia (Osella and Osella 1998, 2002, 2004; De Neve 2004; Nisbett 2004). These approaches have contributed to moving the debate forward by criticizing the individualized and decontextualized notion of autonomy that framed some of the anthropological literature of the 1990s. The theoretical discussion of women's education meanwhile was mainly framed in terms of measuring the impact of education on women's 'autonomy', considered a prerequisite to any other changes (Jeffery and Basu 1996), but the ambiguities implied in the concept of autonomy made it difficult to use it as a reliable indicator of success of education programmes. Evaluations in South Asia have resulted in contradictory findings (Amin 1996; Cleland et al. 1996, Visaria 1996; Caldwell 1996). Autonomy was particularly conceptualized as the link between the frequent finding that mothers with more education had less children but qualititative surveys also showed the difficulty of demonstrating a causal relation between education, women's autonomy and fertility decline (Jeffery and Basu 1996; Jeffery and Jeffery 1998).

My discussion departs partially from the terms of the debate on the impact of education as found in most of the development and policy-oriented literature. In a human development perspective education is seen as having a value in itself but in an efficiency-oriented paradigm women's education is instrumentally linked to broader goals. As Subrahmanian argues, in this perspective, a causal link is assumed between education and 'improvements in wealth, child survival and health ... and declines in poverty and fertility' (2002, 37). More educated girls are assumed to marry later and to be more in control of reproductive choices (Jeffery 2005). In a different approach endorsed by UNESCO and UNICEF, among others, education for women is a prerequisite for more strategic and substantial changes in gender relations in line within a gender mainstreaming perspective. The achievement of gender justice requires a shift from considering gender parity to gender equality. Assessing gender equality ultimately means 'assessing whether fundamental freedoms and choices are as equally available to women as they are to men' (Subrahmanian 2006, 10) and this resonates with the Millennium Development Goal number 3: 'promote gender equality and empower women' (UNESCO 2009a; UNESCO/UNGEI 2005).[2] This goes beyond ensuring equality in enrolment, to focusing on attendance, completion and repetition (Subrahmanian 2006). In this perspective the notion of education itself also needs to be unpacked and problematized, by looking at different types and levels of education and schooling. The need to evaluate the content of the curriculum and the values and norms that the school promotes has also been stressed (Stromquist 1995; Longwe 1998; Subrahmanian 2002, 2006).

Demographic and policy-oriented research in Bangladesh has dealt with the complex intertwining between girls' education, poverty, marriage and the practices related to marriage such as dowry, focusing mostly on primary and secondary schooling (up to 10th grade) and exploring the rationale behind parents' choices in respect to their children's marriage and education (Amin and Huq 2008; Mahmud and Amin 2006; Schuler et al. 2006; World Bank 2008; Hossain 2005; Amin, Selim, and Kamal Waiz 2006; BRAC 2006). Comparative data show that globally there has been progress towards closing the gender gap in enrolment in primary and secondary education. In 2006, out of 176 countries, 20 more than in 1999 reached the target (UNESCO 2009a). Bangladesh has performed particularly well as the only country in South and West Asia besides Sri Lanka to have achieved the Education for All gender parity goal (UNESCO 2009a). The literacy rate has been rising since the early 1990s – 56% in 1999 compared to 24% in 1991 (Economist Intelligence Unit 2005) – and the disparity in the level of schooling between rural and urban areas and between males and females has been narrowing. In 2005 there were more girls than boys enrolled in grades 6–10: 52.8% of girls against 47.2% of boys (BANBEIS 2006).

Some studies (Caldwell 1998; Amin 1996, 1998) have suggested a correlation between the significant increase in girl's enrolment in primary and secondary education and a trend to postponing marriage. The median age at marriage among women aged 20–49 has increased by one year over the past decade, from 14.2 years in 1996–1997 to 15.3 years in 2006–2007 (NIPORT 2009). The statistics also show that more educated women tend to marry later: those who have completed secondary or higher education marry two years later than those with no education. Residence and economic condition also matter: women from the highest wealth quintile marry two years later than those from the lowest wealth quintile and urban women age 25–49 tend to marry one year later than their rural counterparts (NIPORT 2009). However, Amin and Huq point out that 'compared to the impressive improvement in the proportion of girls enrolled in school the increase in the age of marriage is minimal' (Amin and Huq 2008, 6). While on the one hand education seems to have a role in postponing marriage for girls, at least to some extent, the imperative of marriage and the social norms that regulate it seem to be precisely what prevents parents from investing more in their daughters' education. This also appears to be one of the main reasons why girls drop out of school at a faster rate than boys in the two last years of secondary school and in the two years of higher secondary (Mahmud and Amin 2006; Amin, Selim, and Kamal Waiz 2006). It is at secondary level where there has been substantial growth in enrollment and where also dropout rates are very high. In 2005 11.24% of girls dropped out in grade 6, 13.48% in grade 7, 15.9% in grade 8, 35.5% in grade 9 and 47.41% in grade 10 (BANBEIS 2007). Despite the increase in the age of marriage, this is still the lowest among the developing countries included in the Demographic and Health Surveys, and this stands somewhat in contrast to the declining fertility rates and high use of contraception (Amin, Selim, and Kamal Waiz 2006).

In this paper, after a brief discussion about the complex factors that influence parents' decisions about secondary education and marriage for their daughters in my study area, I will focus on college-going girls. These are only a minority, but I argue that it is for them that education has the potential of opening up real spaces for a more complex and articulated transition to adulthood and for differentiated life trajectories. In rural Bangladesh every individual is attributed a defined position and entitlements inside a net of hierarchical relationships as member of the *samaj* (society or moral community), of a group of *attiyo swajan* (literally one's own people), of a lineage or a caste, of a *bari* (extended family), and finally of a *songsar* or *parivar* (nuclear family). Young people experience and confront the process of transition to adulthood in a context shaped by social norms and expectations that predefine their life trajectories and do not encourage them to express their feelings and desires and to take initiatives in forging their lives.

On the other hand, going to college implies the redefinition of one's relational world and the opening up, outside the boundaries of the parental family and the village of new and egalitarian forms of peer and cross-gender interaction. Passing matriculation exams at the end of high school and accessing higher secondary education constitute for girls a significant life event and a significant turning point. My ethnography shows that unlike their younger counterparts who stop studying in order to get married, girls who enrol at college develop more complex and differentiated aspirations for the future. They expect to gain the skills and knowledge that would open for them the doors of paid employment, but, more importantly, prolonged education becomes for them an instrument of personal growth and self-affirmation that potentially strengthens their self-confidence as individuals capable of agency. I use Gramsci's concepts of contradictory consciousness and fragmentation of common sense to disentangle the apparent contradiction between girls' compliance and their desire for independence and the coexistence in their experiences of a strong drive towards 'development' as much as an attachment to 'culture'.

A note on fieldwork

I conducted the fieldwork on which this paper is based for my doctoral thesis from October 2001 to April 2002 and again from October 2002 to April 2003.[3] I conducted the research in three main sites in the district of Satkhira in South West Bangladesh: the village of Tarapur and two colleges, Begum Rokeya and Tagore (one for girls only and one mixed), in Tala. This is the small urban centre after which the sub-district is named and comprises a market, a few government offices, three Intermediate colleges, one Degree college and four high schools. I also visited occasionally a high school in Tarapur and a nearby village called Chadnagar were I had lived for four months in 1980–1981. I adopted a range of methods including participant observation, informal interviews and conversations with adolescent girls aged 14–20, some of whom were studying and others married or waiting to get married; parents; teachers; non-governmental organization (NGO) officers and beneficiaries. I also participated in some wedding ceremonies and other significant social events. I used a structured questionnaire to collect some basic information about the socio-economic structure of the village where I lived and the level of education of the households and another one to collect data about the socio-economic position of the students of the two colleges. In my thesis and in this paper I have changed the name of the villages, of the two colleges and the names of all the people I mention.

My knowledge of spoken Bengali allowed me to enjoy direct and immediate communication with both adults and young people. I paid frequent visits to the high school situated in Tarapur and to the two colleges and I had conversations with the girls in their room in the college and with the boys mainly in the courtyard during their hours off. My work was facilitated by the courtesy and availability of the two principals and the teachers who allowed me free access to the students. At Tagore I ran spoken English tutorials in the first period of fieldwork, as a way of getting to know some of the students. At the beginning I was addressed as 'madam' by both boys and girls during the English classes and as 'auntie' by the girls during the more informal conversations we had in their room. As a foreign 'madam' I was the object of respect and curiosity; as 'auntie' I slowly became for some girls a confidant. The conversations in the girls' room were often very intimate and warm. We talked about a range of issues including their relationships with their parents and their perception of society, their relationships with boys, and their expectations and hopes for the future. They talked quite openly, especially when they could do so indirectly (for example by referring to another classmate who was not present), and sometimes they would just make jokes or sing. Since I was perceived as someone that would not judge them, they felt that they could express themselves openly and frankly. The male college students were also quite curious and willing to talk. The fact that I was not considered a member of the *samaj* (society or moral community), but was literate enough about their society, encouraged dialogue and nurtured relationships of trust. I also visited the girls' and boys' homes in Tarapur and in other villages of the area and met their parents and neighbours. Many informal discussions took place sitting on the veranda of a house, with all the neighbours around and the children screaming, or sitting in a van on the way home, or during NGO meetings that I observed, or sitting in the school courtyard and watching a football match between student teams and so on. All of this was quite time consuming but the conversations proved to be rich and insightful.

In Tarapur there are only a primary and a high school, teaching up to grade 10. For higher secondary studies boys and girls from Tarapur and other villages of the area have to move to the Intermediate colleges in Tala that they reach by bus, bicycle or rickshaw. Here, besides Tagore and Begum Rokeya, there is another college. Tagore is a mixed-sex institution. It offers a two-year course (11th and 12th year) after which the students obtain a Higher Secondary Certificate in Arts, Science or Commerce. It is situated approximately five miles from Tarapur in Tala urban area. It was founded in 1995 by the director of a local NGO, but is now legally recognized and partly funded by the State. Students from Tala sub-district travel daily to reach the college, because there is no hostel. Begum Rokeya College is a girls' college and offers the same higher secondary certificates as Tagore, plus a degree course in Arts, Science and Commerce. It is situated in Tala too and was also founded as a private institution by a group of teachers. It is now recognized and receives funds from the State. Like Tagore, it tries to motivate poor households especially to enrol girls, giving basic textbooks free of charge to the poorest. In both colleges low-fee supplementary classes, run by the same teachers, allow essential extra tuition even for poor students who would not be able to afford widely used private tuition. The college hostel is for degree students only. Education is in Bengali in both the colleges. Intermediate college students' age should be 16 for 11th-year students and 17 for 12th-year students; however a student's career is not always straightforward and college students can be two or three years older. In October 2001, when I started my fieldwork, there were approximately 300 students registered in the first and second years in the Tagore College, of which just 30 were female. In the other college there were about 250 girls but most of them, as I was told, did not attend the lessons regularly and some of them were never present. Around 30% of the girls were married. Out of 150 enrolled in the second year, only 82 filled in the forms to sit the final exams; 75% of the students of the two colleges are Muslim and 25% Hindu by religion.

Staying on at school, class and marriage

A number of recent qualitative studies on early marriage suggest that for girls in rural Bangladesh decisions about education are closely intertwined with the centrality of getting married. Marriage appears in all these studies as the main reason girls drop out of school. The dowry the girl's family has to pay to the bridegroom's family increases with the age of the bride and this is one of the reasons why girls from poorer families tend to marry earlier (Rozario 2002; Amin and Huq 2008; Mahmud and Amin 2006; Amin, Selim, and Kamal Waiz 2006). In my study area, there are strong social norms about the value of marriage for girls, and families and parents make decisions that must navigate the complex ways in which education is useful, or not useful, to the central issue of a girl's marriage prospects (Del Franco 2006). Education is very clearly perceived by adults as being positive and is valued for many reasons irrespective of age and class. Being uneducated (*oshikkito*) is often associated with poverty and with living in a rural area. Being educated (*shikkito*) is deemed to be a quality that can make a real difference in life. Violence and antisocial behaviour are often associated with people who are considered *oshikkito*, who are also considered less in control of their emotions and less rational. Adults endorse a view of education as a means to 'enlighten' both the individual and the society. Educated people are believed to be better, more open-minded and able to bring about positive changes in society. However, the perceived advantages of education are different for boys and girls.[4]

As soon as a girl is considered *boyoshko*, after menarche and sometime even before it, her family may start receiving marriage proposals for her. Poor parents whose daughters are not attending school are likely to consider these proposals seriously. Others may refuse them on the basis that their daughters are still studying, despite some worries about what people might think: 'the *samaj* will say... such a big girl and still at home, there must be something wrong with her, she must have done something bad'. Neutralizing the social pressure and the gossiping about a girl's unmarried state is difficult, but it is not impossible as long as a girl is still studying. This is a justification for girls remaining unmarried used by rich and poor parents alike. Parents may have other reasons for wanting to escape the *samaj* pressure for a time without openly contesting it, for example, while waiting for a better suitor for their daughter, or to accumulate the money to pay for her dowry. Even those parents who can afford to pay for secondary or post-secondary education seem to be mainly concerned about enhancing the possibility of a good marriage for their girls. The perception of the limited local employment opportunities discourages them from investing in girls' education. Being employed as teachers or NGO workers in programmes run by local NGOs is considered by the adults I talked to as one of the possible available forms of employment for women in the area. However, as I was told, matriculation and sometimes nine years of schooling are enough to be eligible for these kinds of jobs. Although work in garment factories has become through the 1990s and 2000s an important source of employment for women, none of the adults or young people I talked to mentioned it as a possible employment opportunity. This might be due to the considerable distance of Tala upazila from Dhaka and other export processing zones (EPZ) and also to the fact that working in garment factories is not perceived as something that would suit an educated girl. To my knowledge only one woman from Tarapur had migrated to Dhaka to work in a factory. Amin (1998) and Amin, Selim, and Kamal Waiz (2006) discuss extensively paid work in garment factories in relation to girls' age at marriage. The latter interestingly point out that 'despite the million strong female workforce in this sector and their propensity to delay marriage in order to work, the impact of these workers on the national average age at marriage is insignificant' (Amin, Selim, and Kamal Waiz 2006, 9). Others studies show that female garment workers come mainly from poor or impoverished landless households (Naved, Amin, and Newby 2001).

In 2002 I conducted a participatory assessment of poverty in Tarapur where the villagers themselves divided the households into four categories according to their level of poverty: *barolok* (rich, well off), *majhari* (middle level), *garib* (poor), *bikka garib* (extremely poor). In what follows I refer to this classification in presenting some examples of parents' attitude towards their daughters' education.

For better off/*barolok* households their daughters' education becomes mainly an enhancer of status, and marriage can be postponed until higher qualifications such as HSC (Higher Secondary Certificate) or a university degree have been obtained. Shirin's family is an example of this. Shirin's mother, besides being busy trying to keep a number of boys away from her girls, was also very worried about the poor school results of Shirin and her older sister. She said:

> I am very worried about the two of them, they do not want to study, we have to force them. All our relatives are educated [then follows a list of relatives and their study achievements]. If they do not manage to get the certificate we will become the last ones.

Throughout 2002 and 2003, Shirin's parents received several marriage offers for Shirin but they dismissed them all. Shirin told me once that her parents had lied, telling everyone that she was not *shekna* (mature) yet.

For households of a lower socio-economic background, those defined as *majhari*, sending a daughter to high school after the five years of primary education seems to be a socially acceptable way of delaying her marriage in order to find a better partner for her in the future. Renu was registered in class 10 at the local high school but throughout my stay in the village she had been working in the fields or helping her mother at home rather than studying. She did not sit the final Secondary School Certificate (SSC) exam in 2003 and after that, for over a year, her brothers had been busy looking for a husband for her. Eventually she was given in marriage in 2004. Her parents were financially able to pay for her study, but felt it was no longer worthwhile.

Girls belonging to more vulnerable households, such as those that have been ranked as 'poor' or 'extremely poor' are likely not to attend school for more than a few years because their parents will try to marry them as soon as possible and normally then requiring less dowry. When the immediate costs of educating girls are directly compared with the costs of a dowry, even if the latter is normally higher, it is considered a more secure investment for the future. I was told by a group of NGO[5] women members that very poor girls will probably have no other choice but to marry a poor peasant, sharecropper or daily labourer who will very likely be illiterate. In this case, if the bride had some years of schooling, her status would be too high compared to that of her husband and her education could become an obstacle instead of an advantage for her and her family. It is in these cases where the preference for educating sons becomes more apparent.

This could also partially explain why many girls, like Renu, are withdrawn from school just before sitting the final exam at the end of the first secondary course. Obtaining the SSC certificate might make a marriage match more difficult. This was confirmed by a group of college teachers who said that parents try to get their daughters through the secondary school course, or at least up to the 10th year of schooling, because this will enhance their possibility of a good marriage. However, most of the girls are withdrawn before they get the final certificate because this could instead be an obstacle to marriage. The final SSC exam is also considered quite difficult to pass and this perception is supported by official statistics: the pass rate was 35.22% in 2001, 40.66% in 2002 and 35.91% in 2003 (BANBEIS 2007).

A group of college teachers:

They will be able to say and let everybody know that their daughter is studying in class 8 or 9 and they will start receiving interesting marriage proposals. At the same time they will be able to save some money for dowry or for buying some gold ornaments with the stipend.[6] They won't spend so much on books because they are not actually interested in their daughters' learning. Before the SSC exam they will marry their daughters off because they know that anyway they won't pass the exam. In this way they won't have to pay the exam fee.

The decision to support girls' education, including secondary and higher secondary school, is thus bound up in complex ways with finding an appropriate marriage partner. After puberty girls are not always inevitably married off, but their lives follow different trajectories in the interlinked educational and marriage careers. As my case studies show, the socio-economic condition of the family matters a lot with respect to these trajectories, to when girls marry and to their level of schooling especially at the two extremes of the socio-economic ladder.

In the second year of fieldwork, I distributed a questionnaire in the two colleges to assess the socio-economic position of the students. I collected information on the sources of income; the quantity of land owned, sharecropped (in and out) or mortgaged (in and out); the level of education of the members of the household. The questionnaire included a question that asked the students to self-assess their situation. Five options were given: (1) very poor, overall situation very bad; (2) poor but able to survive in some way; (3) poor but able to satisfy basic needs; (4) middle level (*majhari*); (5) rich (*dhoni*).

Most of the girls enrolled at Tagore (14 out of 20) come from *majhari* households, four from the second category and only two consider themselves very poor. In the girls' college I could only manage to distribute the questionnaire to 83 girls out of about 250 registered in the first and second years. Of them, 62 defined their households as *majhari* or *dhoni*, 13 considered themselves poor but able to satisfy basic needs, seven poor, and only one extremely poor. The results of this small investigation confirm that proceeding to higher secondary education is clearly conditioned by class for girls.

Only a minority of girls sit the final exams in year 10 and proceed to Intermediate college and university. The national statistics show that the highest dropout of girls is in the 9th and 10th year of secondary school (35.5 and 47.41%, respectively) and that only a minority go on to higher secondary education at Intermediate colleges: in 2005 the gross enrollment rate in grades 6–8 was 67.52%, it was 40.53% in grades 9 and 10 and in grades 11 and 12 at Intermediate colleges it was as low as 11.37% (BANBEIS 2007). The tertiary enrollment rate for males and females was 6% in 2005, of which 24% were females (UNESCO 2009b).

Bangladesh Demographic and Health Surveys for 2004 and 2007 show that median age at marriage is higher for more educated women (NIPORT 2009) and it can be said that students who pass the matriculation exam and enroll in higher secondary education are more likely to marry later and experience a longer period of transition to adulthood than those who get married before completing the secondary school course. Girls attending the last years of high school with the perspective of stopping their study before or soon after matriculation are aware to a great extent that education is not going to make a significant difference in their lives. During conversations with a group of such girls attending eighth or ninth grade, I asked them to tell me how they saw their future. A typical response was 'we will cook at our in laws'. They also confirmed that the main reason why girls stop studying early is mainly *samajik* (social). In this regard they also drew a clear line between town and village life, presenting them as two different environments and two different worlds. 'In town it would be different but in the village you have to get married soon. If we could study in town, it would be possible for our parents to escape the pressure of the *samaj*, but in a village this is impossible'.

Going to college: what kind of new world?
Education and 'independence'

In this section I start by considering how education is valued by the college-going students. I then explore the extent to which education brings critical changes concerning young women's expectations and aspirations for the future in the spheres of work and marriage.

Students share their parents' 'enlightenment' perspective of education. As Prodip (a boy) said:

> if a boy and a girl have a relationship and they do not get married, the girl's reputation will be damaged forever ... this happens especially in the rural areas because people are less educated and they lead a 'low' (*nimno*) life.

Educated people are presumed to be more sensible and reasonable. Education is seen to be bringing about a change of attitude and something that could make the relationships between parents and children easier and less unbalanced. A certain level of education is also associated with a less authoritarian behaviour of parents towards children and youth that allows the latter more autonomy in important life choices. For some, this widens the possibilities for boys and girls to choose their marriage partners.

Prodip (boy): Uneducated parents marry off their daughters soon because they do not know about the health risks they might be subjected to because of early pregnancies...

Zahid (boy): Educated sons respect their parents more, and are more likely to be listened to by them and to be able to express an autonomous choice in case of marriage.

Onup (boy): Educated people are more open minded, can discuss and be interested in different issues, are less emotional and less prone to violence.

Areef (boy): I now see a lot of difference from what I used to see in the village when I was little. Now I see a lot of change in people's attitudes, and in religion and people's beliefs.

Ramesh (boy) referring to two of his neighbours: All the time I saw them having trouble and worried. I thought this was not good. If they had studied they could have set up a small business and they would have not have got married so early because they would have had a better understanding of what they wanted. For all these reasons I think that studying is useful.

For some of the students of Begum Rokeya College, education is a way of acquiring general knowledge that will help them to fulfil better their family roles. For example Lota said: 'If we were educated we could do more in terms of the development of our country and of our family. We would be able to raise our children in the right way and teach them'. This view is in line with another point that some girls stressed about education as providing better social skills to become full members of the society: '*somaje mixte parbo*' ('we will be able to be part of the society'). I was told by some students, who before college had attended Islamic *madrasas*, that being able to mix in society means to know and respect its norms and conform to Islamic precepts. In this sense the ability to integrate is equivalent to the capacity 'to understand' (*bujha*),[7] understood as capacity to know and to conform to social norms. Other students, however, in attributing value to education emphasised that being able to be part of society means knowing how society works and understanding basic social dynamics. This understanding means people are 'not cheated', and are 'able to take one's own decisions' and 'make one's life better'. Here, the improved capacity to 'understand' is conceived as leading to a more active form of agency. In other words, the capacity to know and manipulate social norms to pursue personal goals and not just as a function of adjustment and conformity.

There is a clear connection between education and employment in students' words. The immediate answer I received during group discussions with girl college students about the importance of education was that this could be a means to achieve a settled position ('*protistito howar jonno*') in terms of employment and economic independence. This desire for independence (*shadinota*) was also expressed in terms of 'standing on their own feet' ('*niger pa darano*'). This depended on finding a job after school. Girls expressed a sense of self-esteem and self-worth in declaring their willingness to 'find a job' after finishing their studies. When I asked what they were planning to do after college they said: 'we will get a degree and then a masters degree'. When I asked if they were sure that they would pass the final exams they said:

> of course we will, that is why we decided to come to this college. The teachers are good and we are doing our best. Why should we not pass? If we do not, we will sit the exam again. Then we will go to study at Khulna or Jessore or at the least at Kumira girls' college.[8]

They saw their future employment as the result of their own efforts and expressed self-confidence about being able to acquire the skills needed to find an occupation. Many of them said that they wanted to become teachers or college professors, others nurses. Thus employment seemed to constitute an important terrain for self-expression and self-realization.

To verify what it means in terms of future life choices and what real opportunities are opened to girls that pass the Intermediate exams I identified from school records those girls who had completed the final Intermediate exams at Tagore from 1997 to 2002 and gathered information about their current occupations (see Table 1).

Table 1. Present occupation and marital status of girls who passed or failed the final exam between 1997 and 2002 at Tagore College.

Exam and marital status	Employment status				
	Work	Study	Work and study	Housewives	Total
Pass ($N = 32$)					
Married	1	8	1	4	14
Unmarried	1	10	2	5	18
Fail ($N = 31$)					
Married	1	0	0	17	18
Unmarried	0	0	0	13	13
Total	3	18	3	39	63

The most obvious finding is that only five of the 32 girls who obtained the HSC were employed as well as one of the 31 girls who failed. Out of 63 girls that sat the final exams, a large number (39) were housewives. The majority (18 out of 32) of the girls who passed the final exams were enrolled at a degree college not far from Tala.

As Mamtaj, a bright second-year student said, 'girls do not have much choice, boys can go anywhere, to Dhaka or Khulna to study, they can move freely. Our choices are much more limited, we can study at the university only if we have relatives living in town'. Unlike boys, girls are not usually allowed to move to town on their own, because it is considered dangerous for their reputation and security. So unless they can join an uncle or an elder brother or another relative they tend to study in local colleges, many of which do not offer honours degrees and are therefore less valued.

The students' aspirations then may appear, and in some ways are, dreams rather than realistic expectations. The girls are actually aware of the difficulties in finding a job consistent with their level of education. Despite this, I find what emerges from their words significant for a different reason: in them, the girls are saying that they can imagine their lives and themselves not only as mothers and wives, whose interests and needs are embedded in those of their families, but also as active participants in wider networks of social relations.

The strength of their aspirations and their motivation was evident to me not only through what was being said but even more through what I observed of their daily lives. In particular, I was struck by the determination with which many girls were trying to overcome all kinds of difficulties and obstacles. This was particularly evident in the cases of poorer girls (and boys). For Taslima, for example, whose father took a second wife and left her and her mother, going to school was like running an obstacle race. To reach the college she had to walk for more than half an hour, cross a river by boat and then take a rickshaw or the bus. At home she helped her mother sewing clothes and doing other domestic chores. She was not in a position to pay for private tuition and was therefore under the continuous threat that if she failed an exam, she would be given in marriage. There was strong pressure from relatives and neighbours to get her married quickly. Taslima, her mother and her grandmother were always under observation by their neighbours, and needed to battle constantly to balance their need for work and mobility with the need publicly to adopt a reserved attitude so that people would not gossip. If it had not been for the foreign family that supports her, Taslima would not have been able to fund her studies even if she was highly determined: 'I have a lot of dreams, I will become a good person, I'll get a job, then my father and mother will give me in marriage'. Poorer girls are also bound to face more difficulties in finding an occupation because of their lack of *jogajog* (social connections). They are aware of this and of the fact that they could end up having very limited choices. Taslima had wanted to study science to become a doctor, but this would have implied too many years of study, as well as studying too far away from home. She is now studying Arts.

Girls from well-off families can afford to think about work, and also the kind of work they wish to pursue. Sonia had argued with her father because she wanted to become a 'manager' while her father wanted her to study to become a doctor. Kea showed even more ambitions when she said that she wanted to become a barrister: 'I want to do something important in my life, so that I will be remembered'.

Being compliant

In an apparent contradiction with their hopes and desire of 'standing on their own feet' and becoming more independent through education, college students, often emphasized their sense of being subject to social constraint by saying *mene nite hobe* (it has to be accepted) or *lok kharap bolbe* (people will say bad things). This was true of both boys and girls. The 'society' (*samaj*) represented by different institutional figures, the elders, the *matobars* (village leaders), the group of *attiyo swajan* (relatives and neighbours) is an important referent of values and norms of behaviour in the hegemonic discourse. What people (*lok*) and society 'may think' or 'say' is very relevant not only for adults and parents but for children as well. Girls are more aware than boys that their lives can be negatively affected by others' judgements and this makes them very concerned about their social reputation and the risks of being given a *durnam* (bad name). Girls thus tended to represent themselves as dependent on and subordinate to adults' decisions. I was perceived as *shadhin* (independent) by girls who talked of themselves as *poradhin* (dependent or subordinate) and sometimes as *bondhi* (tied). Independence, here, was generically associated with the capacity to manage oneself and do things according to one's will and less to the economy sphere. I was told: 'You can manage yourself and nobody will tell you what to do. For example, you chose to come to Bangladesh, we have always to ask whenever we want to do something'.

Sometimes girls associated independence with not being subjected to familial pressure and control in terms of mobility and interaction with boys. Most of them complained that: 'We cannot do what we want, we cannot go where we would like to, especially in the evening. Our parents keep asking us where we go, why we are late and what we are doing. They do not do the same with our brothers'. Girls complained that even when they were allowed to go for a walk in the park with friends, they could not stay for long. Moreover they could meet only with females. In most of the conversations they stressed the difference between town and rural areas in this respect: 'Here we cannot mix freely with boys, we would get into trouble and our parents would marry us off. In town it is possible to mix, but not here'.

Girls expressed awareness of a gender disadvantage in the society and within their households and considered themselves bound to be subordinated as females –'*amader konno bekti shadinota nei*' ('we do not have any personal independence'). They also felt they were subjected to much control and discrimination with respect to the possibility of talking and expressing an opinion. During a discussion in a mixed group, Merhuna pointed out that girls have to be careful not to express too much what they feel because they are in a more vulnerable position: 'even if girls do something good, society will look at them in disapproval (*kharap choke dekbe*), but boys do thousands of bad things and people will say ... "good"'.

The area where a sense of constraint was expressed most forcefully (or most frequently) by girls was that of sexuality and marriage. In referring to these, daughters adopted a discourse where the language that prevailed was a dutiful acceptance of parents' decisions. Taslima, the college student mentioned above, had great hopes about her future as an employed woman, but her attitude to her marriage was much more conformist: 'I will finish studying, I will get a job and then my parents will choose a husband for me'. She said that she could not choose on her own because 'in our "culture" this is not acceptable'. 'Culture' more than '*dharma*' was frequently referred to as the ultimate justification for unquestionable and taken-for-granted practices or norms of behaviour. The areas of sexuality and marriage are represented here as beyond discussion and seemed to be the most sacrosanct. This was true for Muslims as well as for Hindus.

Shompa was a wealthy Hindu girl. I saw her behaving in quite a free and self-confident manner at school while she talked with her classmates and teachers, and as she journeyed home with some of her acquaintances. Being Hindu she would not wear *burqa* but she used to keep a 'modest' attitude in the street. For example, she always walked with her gaze looking downwards. Over the time I knew her she voiced contradictory views about her marriage saying on one occasion that she did not want to get married because she wanted to be independent (*shadhin*), but on another that she would accept her parents' will, because they had done a lot for her and borne great hardship.

The discourse of compliance does not mean that the students always expressed complete harmony with their parents. On the contrary, they were aware of generational distance from them. During a group discussion with a mixed-sex group of students, parents were represented as '*ager lok*' (i.e. people of the past). A group of girls said that previously people did not understand the importance of education. 'They did not know about many things. We want to be different from them'. On another occasion, Tonu admitted that: 'there is not much understanding with my father and mother, a lot of times there is not much understanding'.

Education is represented here, once again, as a motor of social change and, in relation to marriage, an asset that can make girls' voice more valued and worthy of consideration. Some girls said proudly that something is changing in comparison with the past, and they are now in a better position to express their opinion in marriage choices. Moreover, as education is supposed to make youth's opinions and views more worthy of being listened to, even in the arena of marriage, choice of the partner starts becoming an issue, with girls being recognized as deserving more voice in this important moment of their lives.

Education and self-hood

From the discussion so far it appears that in the area of Tarapur there is a strong discourse about the value of being educated. Adults as well as young people associate education with positive social change and modernity. College-going girls' and boys' efforts to acquire skills and qualifications are supported by their parents. Their aspirations are socially legitimate even if, for girls, this implies a partial breaking of *purdah*.[9] Even if the majority of parents do value their daughter's education as a marker of status and in function of marriage, poorer parents like Taslima's mother view it also as a possible source of economic independence for their daughters, especially if their marriages broke down.

In addition, there is in some senses a public recognition of college students and they occupy a specific identity that allows them to articulate publicly their hopes and plans for the future. In expressing their wishes and hopes of becoming economically independent, or at least more responsible and active members of their families and their society, girls are showing a strong sense of self-hood and self-esteem, for example in the ease with which they imagine themselves as adults capable of 'standing on their own feet'. In the strong motivation with which girls try to overcome obstacles and constraints, there is more than the simple awareness that being more educated gives them more choices for marriage partners or for jobs. Unlike the girls interviewed by Jeffery and Jeffery, the students of Tagore and Begum Rokeya College do not attend school just because their parents want them to become more marriageable (Jeffery and Jeffery 1994). They show a strong personal motivation for doing it.

Beside parents' motivations and choices, it is essential to consider and give weight to the meaning that girls themselves attribute to reaching higher levels of schooling and to look at how this influences their self-identity. I suggest that changes brought about by this level of education are *de facto* challenging young people's perceptions of themselves, their aspirations for the future, and their position in the *samaj*. They encourage the questioning of parents' decisions. Although only to a limited degree, young people are contesting their powerless position with respect to adults when they envisage more chances to have their opinions and desires taken into account, for example in marriage choices. This applies to boys as well as girls, since they too are in a subordinate position as far as age hierarchies are concerned.

Whatever meaning their parents attach to education, studying at college with a view of proceeding to university opens for girls a contested period in which they struggle to find a compromise between what the *samaj* expects from them and their own hopes and uncertainties. Listening to girls' own experiences allows uncovering their tenaciousness in pursuing not just economic and material success but also in trying to work out a sense of self-hood and self-worth. As for the Indian students interviewed by Chopra, their voices testify 'the hybrid nature of their existence' (Chopra 2005, 307).

The fact that they seem to be captured between two different worlds is apparent in the contradiction between the discourse of constraint with which most of the female students described their present situation and their compliance in marriage choices, and the determination they showed with their behaviour in pursuing education as a means to gain some 'independence'. It is true that girls, especially the poorest, are relatively powerless, and subject to relations of gender and age that allow them little space for assertion and little time for consultation. They are well aware of the cultural context in which they live and of the limited spaces they have to manifest their preferences. Nonetheless education is discursively gaining importance as an element of social change, and is definitely part of the picture. Not only can going to school delay marriage, it is also perceived as a factor that can increase the possibilities of agency for both girls and boys.

The hegemonic view of marriage as a social bond between two households where individual preferences are irrelevant is linked to a hegemonic view of sexuality, of honour and of gender relations. People refer precisely to the values, norms and cultural referents that pertain to these domains when they refer to *'amader* [our] culture'. This expression is often used as an ultimate explanation for attitudes, behaviours and choices related to sexuality and marriage (see Taslima above). Placing some issues in *'amader* culture' means that they cannot be the objects of discussion and that they have to be taken for granted. Adults and young people appear to distinguish and separate discursively two arenas. The first is a 'modern' arena of 'development', well represented by the NGOs, that includes education, work and employment. Here there are no objections to girls studying and women working, and individual self-advancement and a struggle towards economic well-being are encouraged and legitimate. But this is possible provided that *'amader* culture' is safeguarded so that there are issues that cannot be questioned and barriers in the face of which the development discourse and practices have to step back.

This separation is, however, highly constructed and the relations between the domain of 'our culture' and the modern domain of development work and employment are in practice contested and competing. Despite what people say, and the cultural hegemonic view reflected in public discourses, everyday practices challenge this separation. This is evident, for example, in the way adults deal with young people's premarital relationships. Parents are aware of the existence of a hidden adolescent world of more or less platonic 'love stories' built around love letters, passionate glances and furtive encounters made meaningful by the language of romantic love (Del Franco 2006). However, this parallel world is tolerated as long as it remains invisible and does not openly interfere with the sanctioned public behaviour, thus allowing the hegemonic discourse to keep its consistency and coherence. A female university student I met in Dhaka in 2005 was very conscious about the contrasting pressures she had to bear from her parents:

> They expect me to be a successful student and obtain good marks because they say that I have to improve my skills and find a good job, but I cannot go out with my friends and have a boyfriend because they say that this is against our culture. I don't understand what I have to do and it is difficult for me.

They way college students use veiling is another example of how they manage to blend the modern world of 'development' and 'culture'. They compromise with hegemonic notions of *purdah* by wearing *burqa* (a long coat that covers the whole body including the face and except the eyes) or the veil to make themselves symbolically invisible, while at the same time occupying public spaces such as the college and the street. Girls appeal to their 'culture' to explain why their mobility and contacts with boys are limited and controlled, but on the other hand they are able to name the power unbalance that characterizes gender relations: 'this is a country where men have the power'. They do not consider the possibility of fighting openly and collectively for a transformation, and their answers and solutions are mainly individual, but these examples show that the hegemonic discourse is not all-encompassing and that a developmental modernist perspective in practice challenges what is discursively conceived as beyond scrutiny because it belongs to the 'unchangeable' domain of 'culture'.

However, hegemony is not only challenged from the outside in a questionable dichotomous perspective that would oppose 'tradition' and 'modernity'. It is not a matter of an alternative between an individualistic, liberal perspective according to which education and jobs are valued, but unattainable and remaining 'embedded in structures' like marriage that limit one's 'room for manoeuvre' as Jeffery and Jeffery (1998) argue. My study suggests that, particularly as discourses of development and modernity become available and the transition to adulthood becomes more articulated, also because of prolonged schooling, there are more spaces for young women to elaborate and draw from such discourse and to develop personal expectations in contrast with dominant social norms. This allows us to rethink in a more nuanced way the meaning of social embeddedness and to acknowledge that girls are not just passive enactors of other people's interests and desires.

If it is true that specific social relations produce a certain type of consciousness and perception of one's well-being delimited by common sense, it is also true that this consciousness is always in a Gramscian sense 'contradictory' and that identity and status are always renegotiated in everyday practices. The incoherence and fragmentation of common sense is what impedes a simple reproduction of the hegemonic social order and allows for change. In Williams's words: 'the reality of any hegemony in the extended political and cultural sense is that while by definition it is always dominant, it is never either total or exclusive' (1977, 113). In a Gramscian perspective the subordinate groups may develop a 'critical understanding of self through a struggle of political hegemonies and of opposing directions ... in order to arrive at the working out of at a higher level of one's own conception of reality' (Gramsci 1971, 333).[10] But even before the development of a full critical consciousness and of a collective political movement, the subordinates are not merely resistant, they can rather be active, even if in 'weak' and constrained position.

Gramsci's concepts of contradictory consciousness and fragmentation of common sense offer a way forward out of the dichotomy between considering girls fully submerged in a constraining social structure and unable to see where their interests lie, or romanticizing their dreams and their limited individual resistance. It allows a nuanced understanding of the changes that education is bringing about. By prolonging in temporal terms the transition to adulthood and by reinforcing girls' sense of self-worth and self-esteem, education contributes to develop girls' awareness of their own wishes and needs, thus increasing their capacity to negotiate their own ways of being part of the *samaj*. This kind of agency resonates with a dynamic view of gender relations where individuals are conceptualized as capable of self-reflection, and where bargaining, negotiation and conflict are always present (Whitehead 1981; Kandyjoti 1988; Mc Leod 1992; Jeffery and Jeffery 1996; Sen 1990; Mohanty 1988).

Notes

1. College means here Intermediate college that comprises grades 11 and 12. Primary education comprises grades 1–5. Secondary education is divided into first secondary and higher secondary. First secondary education comprises grades 6–10. At the end of grade 10 the students have to sit for a final exam; if they pass it they obtain a Secondary School Certificate (SSC). Grades 6–10 are attended at so-called high schools. Higher secondary education comprises grades 11 and 12. At the end of the 12th year, the students have to pass a final exam to get a Higher Secondary Certificate (HSC). A regular student would start high school (grade 6) at the age of approximately 11 or 12 and finish high school at approximately 16 or 17. The two-year Intermediate college course corresponds in timing to the sixth form college of the English school system.
2. The 2007 World Development Report *Development and the Next Generation* also stresses the importance of developing the 'capacity of young people as decision making agents' (2007, 53) in the five main transitions they go through: learning after primary school, starting a productive working age, adopting a healthful life style, forming a family, exercising citizenship. The World Development Report acknowledges also these transitions are gender differentiated since puberty (2007, 65).
3. My fieldwork was funded by the Simon Population Trust.
4. Del Franco (2006) extensively discusses parents' perspectives on boys' education and its role in their employment opportunities. White-collar jobs, *chakri*, are particularly valued.
5. There are several big and small local NGOs in the area, funded by national and international donors. They run projects for poverty alleviation (microcredit, agricultural extension, health and sanitation) and promotion of human rights. They also work with women by organizing them in groups of about 15–20 members. There is an extensive literature on the role of NGOs in Bangladesh (see Devine 2003, 2009; Lewis and Siddiqi 2003; Lewis 2004; Khan, Ahmad, and Quddus 2009).
6. This refers to the sum paid biannually by the government to girls with good school results up to 12th grade.
7. See Ahmed (2004) for a discussion of the notion of 'understanding' (*bujha*).
8. Kumira College is a simple degree college situated in Kumira, not far from Tala. It constitutes the closest alternative for girls who for different reasons cannot afford to go to Satkhira, Khulna or Jessore.

9. Purdah, which literally means curtain, has not to be understood only in the limited meaning of the physical seclusion of women inside the house. Both for Hindu and Muslims purdah entails an ideal of modesty enforced through 'prohibition on movement, gesture, speech and association and the development of feminine characteristics like virtue and shame' (Ahmed 1993, 60). Papanek argues that purdah operates through two different principles: 'separate worlds' and provision of 'symbolic shelter' (1982, 6). The first is mostly related to the division of labour and a series of rules regarding the use of space. The second underlines the tension between the private domain pertaining to women and the outside world.
10. The 'resisting' individual is for Gramsci a phase in a process: 'if yesterday (the subaltern element) was not responsible, because resisting a will external to itself, now it feels itself to be responsible because it is no longer resisting but an agent necessarily active and taking the initiative' (1971, 337). Resistance for Gramsci presupposes limited awareness and responsibility, and a sort of passive reaction; it presupposes not a false but a contradictory consciousness. Agency is, on the one hand, a transformatory one that implies a collective will, a political action in the perspective of changing the structures of subordination. Does this means that outside a perspective of structural transformatory change for Gramsci there is only mere reactive resistance? Actually it is not so, Gramsci continues the same passage saying: 'but even yesterday was it mere resistance, a mere thing, mere non responsibility? Certainly not. Indeed one should emphasize how fatalism is nothing other than the clothing worn by real and active will when in a weak position' (1971, 337).

References

Ahmed, I. 2004. The construction of childhood in Monipur: Negotiating boundaries through activities. D.Phil. thesis, University of Sussex, UK.

Amin, S. 1996. Female education and fertility in Bangladesh: The influence of marriage and the family. In *Girls' schooling, women's autonomy and fertility change in South Asia*, ed. R. Jeffery and A. Basu, 184–204. London: Sage.

Amin, S. 1998. Family structure and change in rural Bangladesh. *Population Studies* 52: 201–13.

Amin, S., and L. Huq. 2008. Marriage considerations in sending girls to school in Bangladesh: Some qualitative evidence. Working Paper 12, Population Council, Dhaka.

Amin, S., N. Selim, and N. Kamal Waiz. 2006. *Causes and consequences of early marriage in Bangladesh. Background report for workshop on programme and policies to prevent early marriage*. Dhaka: Population Council.

Bangladesh Bureau of Educational Information and Statistics (BANBEIS). 2006. *Bangladesh educational statistics 2005*. Dhaka: BANBEIS.

Bangladesh Bureau of Educational Information and Statistics (BANBEIS). 2007. Educational statistics. http://www.banbeis.gov.bd/db_bb/secondary_ education_2.htm (accessed June 14, 2009).

Bangladesh Rural Advancement Committee (BRAC). 2006. *Adolescents and youth in Bangladesh: Some selected issues*. BRAC Research Monograph Series no. 31. Dhaka: BRAC.

Caldwell, B. 1996. Female education, autonomy and fertility in South Asia. In *Girls' schooling, women's autonomy and fertility change in South Asia*, ed. R. Jeffery and A. Basu, 288–321. London: Sage.

Caldwell, B. 1998. The construction of adolescence in a changing world: Implications for sexuality reproduction and marriage. *Studies in Family Planning* 29, no. 2: 137–53.

Chopra, R. 2005. Sisters and brothers: Schooling, family and migration. In *Educational regimes in contemporary India*, ed. R. Chopra and P. Jeffery, 299–320. New Delhi: Sage.

Cleland, J. et al. 1996. Links between fertility regulation and the schooling and autonomy of women in Bangladesh. In *Girls' schooling, women's autonomy and fertility change in South Asia*, ed. R. Jeffery and A. Basu, 218–34. London: Sage.

De Neve, G. 2004. The workplace and the neighborhood: Locating masculinities in the south Indian textile industry. In *South Asian masculinities: Context of change, sites of continuity*, ed. R. Chopra, C. Osella, and F. Osella, 60–95. New Delhi: Women Unlimited.

Del Franco, N. 2006. Negotiating adolescence in rural Bangladesh: A journey through school, love and marriage. D.Phil. thesis, University of Sussex, UK.

Devine, J. 2003. The paradox of sustainability: Reflections on NGOs in Bangladesh. *The Annals of the American Academy of Political and Social Science* 590: 227–42.

Devine, J. 2009. Organizational success and the informal politics of social change. In *Recreating the commons? NGOs in Bangladesh,* ed. F., Khan, A. Ahmad, and M. Quddus, 107–28. Dhaka: UPL.

Economist Intelligence Unit. 2005. *Bangladesh country profile.* London: The Economist.

Ewing, K. 1991. Can psychoanalytic theory explain the Pakistani woman? Intra-psychic autonomy and interpersonal engagement in the extended family. *Ethos* 19, no. 2: 131–61.

Gramsci, A. 1971. *Selection from the prison notebooks of Antonio Gramsci.* Eds. and trans. Q. Hoare and G. Nowell Smith. London: Lawrence and Wishart.

Haynes, D., and G. Prakash, eds. 1992. *Contesting power: Resistance and everyday social relations in South Asia.* Berkeley: University of California Press.

Hossain, N. 2005. *Inheriting extreme poverty: Household aspirations, community attitudes and childhood in northern Bangladesh.* Dhaka: BRAC and SCUK (Save the Children UK).

Jeffery, P. 2005. Hearts, minds and pockets. In *Educational regimes in contemporary India,* ed. R. Chopra and P. Jeffery, 13–38. New Delhi: Sage.

Jeffery, P., and R. Jeffery. 1994. Killing my heart's desire: Education and female autonomy in rural North India. In *Women as subjects: South Asian histories,* ed.. N. Kumar, 125–71. Charlottesville: University of Virginia Press.

Jeffery, P., and R. Jeffery. 1996. *Don't marry me to a plowman!: Women's everyday lives in rural north India.* Boulder, CO: Westview.

Jeffery, P., and R. Jeffery. 1998. Silver bullet or passing fancy? Girls schooling and population policy. In *Feminist visions of development,* ed. C. Jackson and R. Pearson, 239–58. London: Routledge.

Jeffery, R., and A.M. Basu, eds. 1996. *Girls' schooling, women's autonomy and fertility change in South Asia.* New Delhi: Sage.

Kabeer, N. 2000. *The power to choose.* London: Verso.

Kakar, S. 1978. *The inner world: A psychoanalytic study of childhood and society in India.* Delhi: Oxford University Press.

Kandiyoti, D. 1988. Bargaining with patriarchy. *Gender and Society* 2, no. 3: 274–90.

Khan, F., A. Ahmad, and M. Quddus, eds. 2009. *Recreating the commons? NGOs in Bangladesh.* Dhaka: UPL.

Lewis, D. 2004. On the difficulty of studying civil society: Reflections on NGOs, state and democracy in Bangladesh. *Contributions to Indian Sociology* 38: 299–322.

Lewis, D., and M.S. Siddiqi. 2003. Organizational culture in multi-agency development projects: Lessons from a Bangladesh case study. *The Annals of the American Academy of Political and Social Science* 590: 212–26.

Longwe, S.H. 1998. Education for women's empowerment or schooling for women's subordination? *Gender and Development* 6, no. 2: 19–26.

Mahmud, S., and S. Amin. 2006. Girls' schooling and marriage in rural Bangladesh. In *Research on the sociology of education.* Vol. 15, *Children's lives and schooling across societies,* ed. E. Hannum and B. Fuller, 71–99. Boston: JAI Elsevier/Science.

McLeod, A. 1992. Hegemonic relations and gender resistance: The new veiling as accommodating protest in Cairo. *Signs: The Journal of Women in Culture and Society* 17: 533–57.

Mohanty, C.T. 1988. Under Western eyes: Feminist scholarship and colonial discourse. *Feminist Review* 30: 60–86.

National Institute of Population Research and Training (NIPORT). 2009. *Demographic and health survey 2007.* Dhaka: NIPORT.

Naved, R.T., M. Newby, and S. Amin. 2001. Female labour migration and its implication for marriage and childbearing in Bangladesh. *International Journal of Population Geography* 7: 91–104.

Nisbett, N.C. 2004. Knowledge, identity, place and (cyber)space: Growing up male and middle class in Bangalore. D.Phil., University of Sussex, UK.

Osella, C., and F. Osella. 1998. Friendship and flirting: Micro-politics in Kerala, South India. *Journal of the Royal Anthropological Institute* 4: 189–206.

Osella, C., and F. Osella. 2002. Contextualising sexuality: Young men in Kerala, South India. In *Coming of age in South and Southeast Asia: Youth, courtship and sexuality,* ed. L. Rice Pranee and L. Manderson, 113–31. Richmond, UK: Curzon.

Osella, C., and F. Osella. 2004. Young Malayali men and their movie heroes. In *South Asian masculinities. Context of change, sites of continuity,* ed. R. Chopra, C. Osella, and F. Osella. New Delhi: Women Unlimited (an associate of Kali for Women).

Papanek, H. 1982. Purdah: Separate worlds and symbolic shelter. In *Separate worlds: Studies of purdah in South Asia,* ed. H. Papanek and G. Minault, 1–53. Delhi: DUP.

Raheja, G., and A. Gold. 1994. *Listen to the heron's words: Re-imagining gender and kinship in north India.* London and Berkeley: University of California Press.

Rozario, S. 2002. 'Poor and dark': What is my future? Identity construction and adolescent women in Bangladesh. In *Coming of age in South and South East Asia. Youth courtship and sexuality,* ed. L. Manderson and P. Liamputtong, 42–57. Richmond, UK: Curzon Press.

Schuler, S.R., L.M. Bates, F. Islam, and M.K. Islam. 2006. The timing of marriage and child-bearing among rural families in Bangladesh: Choosing between competing risks. *Social Science and Medicine* 62: 2826–37.

Sen, A.K. 1990. *Gender and cooperative conflicts in persistent inequalities.* Oxford: Oxford University Press.

Stromquist, N. 1995. Romancing the state: Gender and power in education. *Comparative Education Review* 39: 423–54.

Subrahmanian, R. 2002. *Gender and education: A review issue for social policy.* Programme paper no. 3. Geneva: UNRISD.

Subrahmanian, R. 2006. *Mainstreaming gender for better girls' education: Policy and institutional issues.* Kathmandu: UNICEF/UNGEI.

United Nations Educational, Scientific and Cultural Organization (UNESCO). 2009a. Overcoming inequality: Why governance matters. *Education for All Global Monitoring Report.* Oxford: Oxford University Press.

United Nations Educational, Scientific and Cultural Organization (UNESCO). 2009b. *Global education digest.* Paris: UNESCO.

United Nations Educational, Scientific and Cultural Organization (UNESCO)/United Nations Girls' Education Initiative (UNGEI). 2005. *Scaling up good practices in girls' education.* Paris: UNESCO/UNGEI.

Visaria, L. 1996. Regional variations in female autonomy and fertility and contraception in India. In *Girls' schooling, women's autonomy and fertility change in South Asia,* ed. R. Jeffery and A. Basu, 235–68. London: Sage.

Whitehead, A. 1981. I'm hungry mum: The politics of domestic budgeting. In *Of marriage and the market: women's subordination in international perspective,* ed. K. Young, C. Wolkowitz and R. McCullugh. London: CSE Books.

Williams, R. 1977. *Marxism and literature.* Oxford: Oxford University Press.

World Bank. 2008. Whispers to voices: Gender and social transformation in Bangladesh. Bangladesh Development Series paper no. 22, South Asia Sustainable Development Department Dhaka, World Bank.

World Development Report. 2007. *Development and the next generation.* Washington, D.C.: The World Bank.

Aspiring for distinction: gendered educational choices in an Indian village

Nitya Rao

School of International Development, University of East Anglia, Norwich, UK

> Schooling is not a benign process, rather the choice of schooling is often an opportunity for marginalised groups to creatively express particular sets of values in an attempt to gain distinction. Educational attainments carry the potential to open up a range of employment opportunities, but even if these options fail due to structural constraints, particular types of schooling are socially valued for the lifestyles, culture and values they inculcate. This paper, based on field research in Jharkhand, India, explores how people of different social categories make educational choices, focusing particularly on the gendered nature of both their aspirations and strategies for gaining distinction. The experience of state-run schooling is compared to private (including mission) education, both in the locality and at a distance, the latter often perceived to provide higher-quality English education by both parents and children.

Introduction

There is an ongoing debate globally and in India about the types and nature of educational provisioning and its implications on the dynamics of schooling choice and the reproduction of social inequalities (*Compare* Special Issue vol. 36, no. 4, especially Mehrotra and Panchamukhi 2006 and Tooley and Dixon 2006). Most studies contrast state and private provisioning in terms of access, costs and quality, rather than explore student and parental aspirations, and their perceptions about livelihood opportunities and future well-being. The gender-specific ways in which the social and sexual division of labour mediates the schooling experience are largely disregarded. The much coveted white-collar employment is not necessarily an outcome of educational investment due to the presence of other constraints for boys, and often not even an aspiration for girls, yet the choice of a particular school and the prestige attached to it, in itself becomes a marker of social standing and a way of differentiating achievement (Caddell 2006). Schooling choice can simultaneously be used to either reproduce or transform social and gender inequalities, by excluding the marginalised, or providing them an opportunity to gain access to tastes and styles that serve as markers of elite distinction (Bourdieu 1984).

This paper explores how people of different social categories (sex, age, occupation, ethnicity) in a village in Jharkhand, Eastern India, make educational choices, and the way this fits with their distinction aspirations. The village is remotely located, with poor literacy and high poverty rates. It is a mixed-caste village, with populations of

Hindus, Muslims and Scheduled Tribes (STs).[1] Social hierarchies and differences are visible in terms of both educational and occupational status across these categories. Despite the presence of affirmative action and welfare policies in favour of the STs, caste Hindus are doing much better than the other two groups. The Muslims and STs consider attaining education a key strategy to fulfil their aspiration of catching up and competing with the Hindus.

The secondary school certificate in particular is seen as a minimum qualification for most professional jobs, yet in India, few rural boys and girls actually manage to complete their secondary school. At the upper primary level, 50% of enrolled children drop out before completion, with the proportion as high as 65% for ST children (Govinda and Bandyopadhyay 2007). Additionally, given the differential expectations from and aspirations of men and women across these categories, decisions around schooling remain gendered. While Hindu girls, for instance, may seek schooling in order to make a good marriage (cf. Srivastava 2006), for ST girls it may involve the ability to negotiate a better deal at the workplace rather than status considerations *per se*.

Field work for this study was undertaken during July to October 2006, with a follow-up visit in September 2008, as part of a larger project seeking to understand the interlinkages between migration and schooling decisions. All the village households were surveyed to identify occupational and educational patterns across social categories. The population in each social category (Hindu, Muslim and ST) was then stratified by gender (male/female), educational level (below primary/secondary level) and migration status (migrant/non-migrant), into eight sub-categories. Two people were selected for in-depth interviews from each of these sub-categories, where available (for instance, there were no female migrants amongst the Hindus and Muslims in the village, and no secondary level-educated females amongst the STs) to gain a more contextualised picture of aspirations and constraints within particular systems of relationships and practices. Out of a potential 16 interviews from each social category, based on the stratification, a total of 12 interviews were conducted with the STs (eight male and four female), eight with Hindus (four male and four female, all non-migrants) and eight with Muslims (six male and two female). While briefly discussing the schooling experience of the different social categories, the main focus of this paper is on the numerically dominant yet marginalised STs.

In the next sections I briefly set out my theoretical framework drawing on Bourdieu's notion of distinction and the idea of education as a product that can be creatively consumed. After discussing the village context briefly, I use insights and narratives from the interviews to point out how despite the weight of structural constraints, the marginalised attempt to use the schooling process to challenge and transform existing social and economic hierarchies.

Education as a strategy for inter-generational mobility

The experience of schooling is often contradictory: it carries the potential for inter-generational mobility, but it can also contribute to reproducing social and gender inequalities and status hierarchies by justifying privilege and attributing poverty to personal failure (Longwe 1998). Reproduction theorists such as Bourdieu and Passeron (1977) describe how the educational system legitimises the social order and transmission of privilege on grounds of academic certification and merit. Children from poorer and working-class families, from lower castes and tribes, consistently underachieve at every level of the educational system compared to middle- and upper-class children. They are ultimately pushed out of school and this exclusion and their social destiny is then attributed to the lack of merit. The reasons are seen largely as structural rather than personal: lack of state investment in schools attended by a majority of poor children (and rural schools), issues of language, demeaning attitudes of teachers, low expectations of different groups of children and an irrelevant and biased curriculum, as well as poor health and poverty itself (Kumar 1993; Bowles et al. 2005). For girls schools may sometimes provide more progressive models of gender relations than in the family and an escape from domestic work. Dropouts amongst girls are often linked to cultural practices around puberty and marriage, safety and domestic labour, as evidenced by the fact that girls who stay on in school generally end up performing better.

In a fast-changing rural context, where agriculture is no longer sufficient for survival and meeting the aspirations of the youth, migration is a widespread reality. The debates around gender and migration, as around education, have highlighted how outcomes are linked quite closely to one's social positioning as well as the structure of assets – financial, human and social (Mosse et al. 1999; Breman 1985), with the socially and economically disadvantaged doing worse than those with some starting resources. However, geographical mobility does also seem to have a connotation in terms of certain key life skills, including the ability to negotiate and survive in unknown contexts, apart from exposure to new cultures, ideas and ways of living. For women, migration often also provides exposure to less oppressive urban cultures and aspirations that include a transformation in hierarchical gender relations (Jackson and Rao 2009; Unnithan-Kumar 2003).

While differences in economic standing do contribute to the shaping of aspirations and goals, both educational and occupational, of young people, they do not necessarily accept this as a given, but seek other strategies for mobility, often consumption-oriented. Appadurai attributes this largely to the communication revolution – the rapid spread of information and communication technologies over the last decade – be it the internet or mobile phones, bringing in their wake a new global culture, linked to the consumption of different types of goods and services as markers of status. People's experience of movement, of accessing new technologies and ideas has resulted in creating a new landscape of aspirations and practice, what he calls the 'capacity to aspire' (Appadurai 1996, 59).

These larger shifts have led to a decline in the popularity of reproduction as a conceptual tool in the 1990s in favour of a more agentic view of the schooling experience and the ways in which forms of interaction can have both reproductive and transformative potential in particular time-space contexts (Collins 2009). The same applies to an analysis of gender relations, with domination no longer seen as either static or unidimensional, rather giving weight to women's agency in the development process. Evidence can be found in the case of children from less advantaged backgrounds opting for vocational rather than academic courses, as apart from carrying higher risks of failure, the latter may not be best suited for reaching their goals (Erikson and Goldthorp 2002; Rao 2009).

Growing up in environments where there appears to be little hope for mobility, there is a further tendency to rebel against the system rather than conform to it (Willis 1977; Balagopalan 2005). The wife of the ST village headman narrated:

> I would send my son to school each morning, but he would stop and play in the fields or forests and return home in the evening. I did not discover that he had never attended

school till the end of the academic year. The teachers said he had no brains, but I realised that this was linked to the attitudes of the teachers and his lack of understanding of a largely alienating curriculum.

Even individual acts of exclusion/dropout are then linked to the subjective assessment of the chances of success in an educational system that favours the local Hindu elite; in this case the child's actions varied from parental aspirations. The boy now migrates for wage-work; his rebellion has only served to reproduce his class position. Such resistances, however, do have the potential to shift existing norms and practices, not just in the school, but in the wider context of lived experience as demonstrated through several cases in this paper. This is because resistance can take many forms, it is not just rebellion, but students could also appropriate, select, accommodate or generate their own meanings in specific social spheres (Giroux 1983, 83).

Bourdieu's (1984) notion of distinction provides a useful way of understanding how people organise their perceptions of social space and social status in terms of a lifestyle that includes a range of cultural practices such as dress, speech, bodily dispositions, tastes etc. that are socially valued. While he links this to one's own class position (what he calls 'class habitus'), built into the idea of distinction is a notion of mobility. Hence while 'culture' could denote an intrinsic disposition, it is equally something that can be cultivated. Objects similarly are not 'objective' in the sense of meaning exactly what their technical characteristics specify, rather they are given value in the world of social uses and the perceptions people have of its value. Education, in particular schooling, can be considered as a 'product' that helps cultivate particular lifestyles, tastes and dispositions that contribute to distinction, while not denying that the experience of schooling and its outcomes do vary with the type of school one attends, one's class position and more broadly one's ethnic, gender and social identity that places a person within existing social hierarchies (Lynch 1989; Bourdieu and Passeron 1977; Bowles et al. 2005). There is a constant tension between the structural constraints imposed by economic structures, wealth, language and the experience of schooling itself, and the strategies (both conforming and resisting) involved in making it successfully through the system, with pupils also adapting and conforming to school cultures as a way of getting ahead.

While understanding social organisation and positioning owes a lot to Weberian ideas of class, status and power, the idea of distinction helps one break out of these categories, as the strategies for gaining distinction could lie in the realm of ownership and control of property and relations of production, but equally in consumption, social interaction, marriage, or indeed education. Migrant youth often return home with mobile phones and mp3 players, or trousers and shoes, and rather than viewing this as conspicuous consumption, they see it as demonstrating 'tastes' and contributing to distinction, in a context where they remain marginalised within traditional forms of ranking. Similarly, the choice of schooling, in particular, fee-paying private schools, carries within it varying perceptions of quality, of potential networks and opportunities, apart from differential costs (Rose 2009). Consumption here needs to be viewed as a social, cultural and moral project (Miller 1995). The imperatives behind consumption and its experiential aspects emerge as being more than just functionalist, carrying elements of creativity in flaunting one's achievements. While consumption is a marker of social inequality, it can also be a symbol of social success.

New forms of gaining distinction through consumption are now widely visible, yet older forms of cultural capital as reflected in educational attainments have not been given up altogether. When migration is seasonal, less secure and perceived to be a result of desperation or distress, as for the STs in this instance, the earnings contribute to household survival rather than enhancing consumption in any substantial way. The aspiration here is to give up migration, or drastically change the quality of migration, and one of the strategies that could make this possible is an investment in education. Most of the better-educated Hindus in the study village are in fact non-migrants, seeking white-collar jobs locally. Higher levels of education are then seen as a core human capability that can potentially lead to both economic security and social status for households that start relatively poor (Nussbaum 2000).

Gender differences are not explicitly discussed within the ideas of distinction (or indeed reproduction or resistance), yet they are implicitly acknowledged in terms of the differential valuations of roles, and their segregation. In India, amongst the Hindu castes in particular, restrictions on women's mobility forms an important element of social status, hence this becomes an aspiration for other social groups too. The only jobs seen as acceptable for women are white-collar jobs, often in the teaching profession, requiring higher levels of education, and these are few and far between. Educational investments in girls, however, are increasing; this is not so much for them to secure jobs as to find well-off marriage partners, bringing distinction both to their natal and marital households through demonstrating the social graces and practices acquired through schooling. Women's migration for work, while enhancing their personal confidence and sense of autonomy, opening up possibilities for changing roles and activities, for developing new skills and experiences, is however seen to lead to a loss of status for the family.

Village context

Mahari village[2] in Sahibganj district is educationally the most backward district in Jharkhand state, with an overall literacy rate of 37% (Government of India 2001). The village is fairly large with 330 households: 176 ST (primarily belonging to the Santal tribe and some Mohlis or bamboo-workers), 94 Hindu (largely Other Backward Castes, and a few Scheduled Castes) and 60 Muslim households. A railway line set up by the National Thermal Power Corporation (NTPC) to ferry coal from the Lalmatiya coal mines (6 km away in Godda district) to the industrial belt in the neighbouring state of West Bengal divides the village into two. One side is inhabited by the Hindus (who refer to this part as a separate Hindu village) and the other by the Santals, Mohlis and the Muslims. The government middle school, health centre, post office, local provision shops and telephone booth are all located in the centre of the Hindu hamlet. The other side of the village has none of these facilities. The village has no electricity or transportation, though private jeeps do operate from the village on market days.

Occupations here are clearly divided by religion and ethnicity, a microcosm of the segregation found at the all-India level (Sachar 2007, 93). Agriculture and wage labour dominate the occupational profile of the Santals, with the Mohlis engaged in making bamboo baskets for sale. With forest produce now negligible and agriculture at subsistence levels, a large majority of them, both men and women, migrate seasonally to the sugarcane fields of western Uttar Pradesh, or the paddy fields or stone crushers in West Bengal, for an additional income. The Muslims are primarily petty traders engaging with trading livestock, coal, cloth and other household products as well as umbrella repair, though some also migrate to factories in Delhi and Uttar

Pradesh. Muslim women are largely confined to their homes. The Hindus are divided into two groups: the more educated (including the caste groups of Sah, Thakur and Teli) are engaged in teaching, medicine, government jobs or petty contracts; and a large number of the others (Kumhars and other lower-ranked backward castes) are engaged in wage labour, pottery or trading coal. In terms of making a living then, apart from some of the upper-ranked Hindu castes, a majority have insecure livelihoods, moving in and out of the village when the need arises.

A little over 30% of the village population is literate, with 6.5% having completed secondary schooling (grade 10) and less than 1% graduation (Table 1). There are large differences by ethnicity and gender, with literacy rates ranging from about 50% for Hindus to 20% for STs and a dismal 1.5% for ST women. This reflects not just poverty, lack of pupil motivation or parental disinterest to persist with education, as is often suggested, but also the forms of exclusion practised in schools, a major one being the language of schooling (cf. Subrahmanian 2005). While Hindi remains the medium of instruction, a majority of the STs are monolingual in Santali (Government of India 2001), making it difficult for these children to learn.

Attendance remains low amongst the STs and Muslims, a further deterrent being the railway track separating their hamlets from the school, making access difficult. While there is no overt discrimination against ST girls, Muslim girls are largely excluded from schooling. There is a trend amongst these groups to access private or religious educational institutions, mission schools in the case of STs and *madrasas* (Quranic schools) in the case of Muslims. While involving costs, both financial and emotional, they are perceived as sensitive to the needs of the concerned social group, hence providing a more conducive environment for learning.

While the 'consumption' of private education for these groups is almost seen as a necessity, apart from being a mark of distinction, separating as it does those who can afford it and those who cannot, interestingly enough, a majority of the literate Hindus (OBCs and SCs) had attended the local government middle school (up to class 8). After completion, the boys were often sent to the Borio high school to complete matriculation, following which Sahibganj college was a preferred destination for those who continued. It is only in the last few years that a handful of Hindu girls have matriculated from this village. The parents generally expressed a preference for a

Table 1. Literacy levels by ethnicity (population six years and above).

	ST	SC	Muslim	OBC	Total
Illiterate	486 (80)	26 (41)	132 (62.75)	142 (50.75)	786 (67.6)
Primary (1–5)	81 (13)	18 (28)	62 (29.5)	49 (17.5)	210 (18)
Middle (6–8)	19 (3)	10 (16)	10 (4.75)	46 (16.5)	85 (7.5)
Secondary (9–10)	19 (3)	4 (6)	4 (2)	22 (8)	49 (4.25)
Intermediate (11–12)	1 (0.25)	3 (4.5)	1 (0.5)	14 (5)	19 (1.75)
Graduation (13–15)	2 (0.5)	1 (1.5)	1 (0.5)	6 (2)	10 (0.5)
Post-graduation (16–17)	0	0	0	1 (0.25)	1 (0.1)
Not answered	1 (0.25)	2 (3)	–	–	3 (0.2)
Total	609 (100)	64 (100)	210 (100)	280 (100)	1163 (100)

Notes: ST, Scheduled Tribes; SC, Scheduled Castes; OBC, Other Backward Castes.
Figures in brackets are percentages.
Source: Village survey (2006).

functioning and accountable government school system rather than relying on increased marketisation (cf. Harma 2009).

In November 2002, the government set up schools 'on demand' in the ST and Muslim neighbourhoods, under the Sarva Shiksha Abhiyan (SSA) or Education for All programme. As children numbers increased, both these schools were upgraded to Primary Schools in June 2006, and are now listed as New Primary Schools (NPS). While starting with single teachers, two additional teachers, local Muslim educated youth, were appointed in the Muslim hamlet and one more in the ST hamlet, this time an educated Santal man (the earlier appointee being an OBC from the Hindu hamlet). School buildings and infrastructure have been sanctioned – the school building is already in use in the Muslim hamlet and in the final stages of construction in the ST hamlet. There has clearly been an emphasis on improving access and creating the requisite infrastructure to facilitate learning. Midday meals are also provided to the NPS. A cluster resource centre (CRC) has been constructed in the middle school complex (upgraded in 2007 to a high school) and an academic incharge appointed in November 2005 to provide academic support to teachers especially in maths and science. Progress seems to have been made: primary schools set up in each of the hamlets, better infrastructure provided alongside attention to quality through the provision of academic support.

Educational access and distinction: issues and contradictions

Apart from universalising access, the SSA seeks to bridge social, regional and gender gaps, with active community participation in school management. The SSA framework, in thus recognising education as a social institution, which can perpetuate and reproduce inequalities, focuses on critical dimensions of institutional reforms, community ownership, capacity-building, and the role of teachers in the educational process,[3] yet its experience of dealing with social structures or delivering quality education has been uneven. New forms of inequality have emerged even within the structures of the state-run educational system. This has implications for educational choices, as both students and parents are searching for educational opportunities that can help overcome existing structural constraints, failing which they seek alternate strategies for gaining distinction.

Government schools and the new segregation

A marked difference is visible between the three state-run schools in the village. The primary school, located in the Hindu hamlet, was upgraded to a middle school as early as 1971–72, and recently to a high school. The school has eight regular teachers, four buildings, drinking water and toilets, and a computer room, though the lack of electricity has made this non-functional. All ST and SC children receive free textbooks, albeit late, and a scholarship to cover their costs. SC/ST girls in grade 8 are given bicycles by the Jharkhand Education Department to encourage them to continue their studies. Most of the educated in the village have had their basic education in this school. Table 2 provides enrolment figures for 2006 and 2008, pointing to a total withdrawal of Muslim children, explained largely by the existence of a functional and accountable primary school in their hamlet (but also pointing to their absence at post-primary levels), and a fairly stable population from the other groups. Table 3 reveals large increases in the numbers of both ST and Muslim children enrolled in the NPS,

Table 2. Enrolments in the Mahari middle school (grades 1–8).

Caste/ethnicity	Male 2006	Male 2008	Female 2006	Female 2008	Total 2006	Total 2008
Harijan (SC)	11	5	9	6	20	11
Adivasi (ST)	56	84	68	38	124	122
OBC (Hindus)	117	114	100	91	217	205
Muslim	28	0	0	0	28	0
Total	212	203	177	135	389	338

Notes: ST, Scheduled Tribe; SC, Scheduled Caste; OBC, Other Backward Caste.
Source: Information from school (2006, 2008).

Table 3. Enrolments in the two New Primary Schools (2008).

Caste/ethnicity	Muslim school Male	Muslim school Female	Muslim school Total	ST school Male	ST school Female	ST school Total
Harijan (SC)	–	–	–	–	–	–
Adivasi (ST)	38	16	54	41	27	68
OBC (Hindus)	–	–	–	2	5	7
Muslim	62	57	119	–	–	–
Total	100	73	173	43	32	75

Notes: ST, Scheduled Tribe; SC, Scheduled Caste; OBC, Other Backward Caste.
Source: Information from school (2008).

most of them previously out-of-school. The strategy of having schools within hamlets has definitely helped to boost enrolments, and thus meet the objectives of universalising access.

Visits to the two new schools brought out contrasting pictures. While the school in the Muslim hamlet has a proper building, three teachers, a functioning *balwadi* (day-care centre) for three- to six-year-olds and a regular provision of midday meals, the school in the ST hamlet was a complete contrast. The building is yet unfinished, the school officially running in the veranda of the chairperson of the Village Education Committee (VEC). The school has only one teacher, Narain Sah, a Hindu. The chairman said:

> I have called him many times, but he doesn't come. The school hasn't opened for the last three months. He says he has to go to the bank, or to a meeting or file a report. While officially there are 75 children enrolled, there are no studies here. About 20–25 children go to private and mission schools. I send my three children to the mission school. It is expensive, costing almost Rs 4000[4] (GBP 50) per year for each child, but what is the alternative?

Two major issues emerge from the above narrative. While community participation, accountability to the user, choice and consumerism are an important part of the discourse of decentralisation, the existing social hierarchies and power relations limit such accountability and choice (Pryor 2005). Parents, including the VEC, are not easily able to question the teacher or demand accountability from him. Several studies have found teacher absenteeism in government schools to be a major reason pushing the poor towards private education (PROBE Team 1999). There is a second element at play here which relates to dual enrolments. Children are enrolled in the state school with the hope that they can access benefits such as the midday meals, but in the absence of any teaching or learning, parents, a majority of them illiterate, yet recognising the importance of education both in terms of its quality and social functions, decide to enrol them simultaneously in private schools.

Many parents confirmed that the major cash expenditures incurred by them were on health and education. Bitimai and her husband Chotu Soren have some land which they cultivate with paddy during the rains and engage in labouring tasks at other times, earning approximately Rs 3000 per month. Their son and daughter are both enrolled in the local government school, but their son attends the St James School at Pathra. The cost of schooling, including fees, books and a uniform, works out to approximately Rs 500 per month, almost a sixth of their earnings, so they could not afford to send their daughter there as well. Bitimai said, 'I know the local school is not enough for my daughter. Unless this is supplemented with private tuitions, she will not learn anything'.

This indicates the widespread adoption of private tutoring as a supplement to state school provision, with children receiving tutoring likely to perform better and stay longer in school (Bray 2006, 521). It is also cheaper than investing in private education. Chunu Hembrom, a Santal contractor and Chairperson of the VEC of the Mahari high school, is currently educating his son at the Sahibganj college at considerable expense (over Rs 1500 per month for board and fees). His two daughters go to the village school and for an hour's additional tutoring thereafter to a Hindu teacher, costing him Rs 50 per child per month.

Interestingly, and somewhat inexplicably, while the NPS now have permanent infrastructure, the children in the NPS are not eligible for scholarships. When enrolled in the middle school, these children received scholarships; they are now neither entitled to be enrolled in the middle school, nor to scholarships. The headmistress of the middle school, a Santal woman herself, clarified that since the new schools have now been upgraded to primary schools, they each have a clearly demarcated catchment area, and she cannot give admission to children living in the catchment of the ST school, even though she realised that her school was both functional and better resourced than the other. She admitted that the better off amongst the STs sent their children to mission or private schools, but the rest remained out of school. Lack of choice between the state schools had led to a new segregation based on ethnicity.

Narain Sah, the Hindu teacher of this NPS, explained the difficulties he faced in terms of lack of infrastructure, lack of scholarships, but also the attitude of the parents, who preferred to send their children to work or graze cattle than to school, not surprising in a context of extreme poverty. He however admitted that during the period July 2006 to October 2007, when there was a second teacher, a local Santal youth, attendance had improved considerably. I had met Samuel during my visit in 2006, an extremely committed and bright young man, who had educated himself with great difficulty, especially following his father's death in 1989, when he was only 10 years old. As the eldest son, his mother expected him to take over the family farm. He resisted this pressure as he wanted to study, but two of his siblings paid the price. His elder sister was married and her husband came to stay to help with the farm, and his younger brother was pulled out of school to help his brother-in-law. Samuel matriculated in 1995 from a mission school and his graduation was in 2001, yet had been struggling to find a job. According to him, 'I was appointed only as a helper in this school on a 10-year contract, and a salary of Rs 2000 per month. I have to support my family and this is totally insufficient, yet without money to pay bribes I am unable to get a job'.[5] Yet he worked hard in the school, encouraging the children to study, explaining things to them in Santali, till he took up a job as Gram Sevak (village-level worker) responsible for the implementation of the National Rural Employment Guarantee Programme in an adjacent block. Though still on contract, this brings him a better salary.

This then is the second problem with the NPS. As per official notification, the NPS are only ever entitled to hiring para-teachers.[6] Though young, local and better educated, they remain contract workers, with low salaries, and while sincere about teaching, are pushed to finding supplementary occupations in order to make a living. One is a journalist, another an insurance agent, a few give private tuitions to children after school. Shekar Sah and several others (all of them Hindu) admitted that they are only able to teach for half a day, the salary of Rs 3000 per month is insufficient. There has been considerable mobilisation of para-teachers in Jharkhand and negotiations with the government, yet the new guidelines while allowing for an increase in wages to Rs 5100 per month, rule against any future regularisation of tenure. The glaring inequality with the regular teachers, often only matriculation pass, but earning three times this amount, has reduced teacher motivation, central to improving educational quality.

Indeed there is considerable variation amongst the state schools themselves. Under the rubric of universalisation, the poorest have gained access, yet the quality of these new schools remains questionable. Choice is non-existent, as they are excluded from the better resourced and functioning state school, located in the Hindu hamlet. Even though numerically strong, the voice of the STs goes unheard, they are denied benefits, both monetary (scholarships) and in terms of teacher quality. It appears to be in the interest of the elite mediators, both teachers and state bureaucrats, to perpetuate the existing social hierarchies by not adequately redirecting resources to support pupils from the marginalised groups, as this could potentially threaten the interests of the elite (cf. Lynch 1989). To this extent, the state schools do contribute to reproducing social inequality in Mahari.

Yet there is potential for transformation in relations of ethnicity, religion and gender. A clear sign is the large-scale enrolment of Muslim children in the school in their hamlet, in particular girls, and their regular attendance on account of the sensitive teaching and school environment created by the three Muslim teachers, all local youth. During the survey I did not find even a single Muslim woman educated beyond grade 4, now there are several girls entering grade 5. Even if many of them do not pursue further education, completed primary schooling in itself provides them with some knowledge and skills which their mothers lack. Even in the ST hamlet, the potential for change was evident in the brief period when a Santal youth worked as assistant teacher.

While there is no overt gender discrimination amongst the STs, when Samuel left, the children too, both boys and girls, stopped attending. From the perspective of ST parents, the main purpose of education is to improve their children's futures, and provide them the linguistic skills, tastes and social graces that form a sign of distinction, and can potentially contribute to both social and economic mobility (including white-collar jobs). While expressing a preference for state schools, when these fail to meet their aspirations, then ST parents find it worth investing in private (mission) education from early on, even at considerable personal sacrifice. They are often not able to afford private school fees or even supplementary tutoring fees for all their children, and in the process of selection, girls generally tend to lose out. There are currently six or seven Santal boys studying in high school, but no girls at this level.

Moving for education: private education in mission schools

While some Muslim boys do move to *madrasas* in different cities to pursue their studies, and Hindus to cities with private schools, this section focuses on understanding how far the strategy of investing in private education, especially that offered by the missionaries, pays off in terms of status gains for the STs. The example of Samuel who was first appointed as an assistant para-teacher and later secured a position as a Gram Sevak has been discussed above. Most other Santal youth have not been so lucky. Anil Murmu too studied at the same mission school, yet withdrew before his secondary school exams due to ill-health. Once he recovered, he enrolled at the Borio government high school, as his parents no longer had money to send him back to the mission school; a lot had been spent on his treatment. But there was hardly any teaching going on, so he dropped out. In 2005, he travelled to the northern state of Uttar Pradesh with other boys from the village and started working in the sugarcane fields. He stayed there for close to eight months, working on the fields from morning till night, and received a monthly salary of Rs 1000 in addition to food and accommodation. He was frustrated, as despite his education, the only opportunity for work appeared to be as an agricultural labourer, and while manual work on his own land was acceptable, working as a wage labourer seemed humiliating. Anil said, 'it would have been better had I not been educated, at least I would not have felt so bad at the treatment I received. With my education, I had hoped to do better'. This frustration led him to think of other ways in which he could gain distinction, distinguishing himself from others of his social group who had been eliminated from the education system much earlier (Bourdieu and Passeron 1977, 82).

While labouring himself, he used his basic educational skills and the confidence this provided to develop links with other sugarcane farmers, and turned into a jobber (contractor), receiving a commission of Rs 3000 per worker. About half this amount is spent on their transport, railway tickets and other expenses, but the rest is his savings. He took 17 young men last year, and this gave him savings of around Rs 20,000. He has opened a bank account, but also bought a mobile phone – a marker of status, as very few Santals have them, rather it appears to be a privilege of the educated Hindu castes. But it is also useful for staying in touch with the employers and getting a sense of the demand for labour. As a school dropout, Anil knows that he can never get a white-collar job, and with poor social contacts, gaining clients too is increasingly proving difficult, yet he is using his schooling experience to acquire other signs of privilege in terms of dress, speech and a lifestyle. He dreams of saving enough in a few years to buy a motorcycle – once again a symbol of success – knowing fully that this dream can never be fulfilled through cultivation of rainfed paddy alone.

Twenty-eight children of school-going age from a total of around 250 or a little over 11% of ST children are presently going to mission schools, 14 each to the St James Mission School and the Holy Cross Mission School. Except for two who board at the school, most of these children commute daily, walking for more than an hour each way. Fees are high, Rs 400–500 per month, which the parents can barely afford, as these schools receive no state aid. While ST children are entitled to scholarships in government schools, and this is perhaps one reason they stay enrolled, they do not receive them in the mission schools. The headmaster of St James said:

> Four years ago, the Block Development Officer had been approached for minority recognition and monetary help to the school, he promised to help since the government had formulated a policy on recognising mission schools in Scheduled Areas as part of the Education for All initiative. The local RSS[7] activists heard about this and mobilised people in the area against the school and the work of the Diocese. Therefore, the funds did not come through. The only way for us to function is to charge the children some fees to cover basic costs.

The issue does not seem to be one of conversion alone, as a large number of upper-caste Hindus themselves are educated in mission schools. The aim seems to be to maintain their social dominance in the area emerging from their educational achievements, by making such schools, known for their quality, out of reach for the poor.

The *Annual Status of Education Review* (ASER 2007) across Indian states has shown that the quality of education or its relevance is not necessarily better in private schools (Mehrotra and Panchamukhi 2006). It is the discipline enforced on the children and the regularity of teaching which at least makes them both literate and numerate, and able to access opportunities creatively as Anil has done. It moulds them into particular characteristics of distinction, such as forms of dress – shorts, shirt and a tie for boys, with shoes and socks – even though inappropriate to local climatic conditions; in particular forms of speech and linguistic styles such as pronunciation, intonation, phraseology that reflect the social conditions of acquisition and differ substantially from their everyday expression; and in certain sets of values, often alien from their own, though associated with the upper classes in society. So while Anil continues to cultivate at home and work as a labourer outside, he speaks Hindi fluently, sports trousers and a T-shirt rather than the locally used *lungi* (loincloth), carries a mobile phone and aspires to a motorbike. Adopting particular symbols and characteristics of the upper classes he hopes could eventually contribute to a shift in his identity and social standing.

Interestingly, the few secondary school graduates in the older generation such as Chunu, Lakhiram or Babulal too were unable to access government jobs and even though their daily lives were not too different from that of their neighbours, they have insisted on educating their children, based on claims that education has helped their careers and given them a sense of distinction and social standing. One is a successful contractor, one a guard, another a teacher. As Bourdieu and Passeron argue, it is the length of education that allows for the 'internalisation of the principles of a cultural arbitrary capable of perpetuating itself once the training has ceased' (1977, 31) and, it is further secondary school credentials that give recognition to the authority of learning provided by the school, what they call the 'certification effect' (1977, 165). While not necessarily linked to individual capacities, it helps conserve power and privileges amongst the selected few. While primary schooling does have some gains, especially for girls as discussed in the next section, these are hardly sufficient for boys for gaining distinction in society either through educational careers (including the provision of tuition) or by accumulating wealth through becoming a successful middleman or contractor. Male primary school graduates are then confined to activities and sectors that belong to the working classes.

There is another route too to access private education, and that is to send their children to stay with kin and relatives in towns or locations outside the village that may have better schooling opportunities. The Hindus appear to have been more successful in adopting this strategy. Sheila's son studied till class 2 in the local government school, but was then sent to the district town of Pakur to live with her sister for further education in the Torai mission school. She said, 'The studies are much better than in these government schools. The village school does not even teach English. Everything is in Hindi. There is no discipline and teachers show no interest in the students or teaching'. Clearly for Sheila, learning English too was a mark of distinction, and a strategy for keeping ahead of the other social groups in the village.

Amongst the Muslims, the few who are educated, like the three teachers, received free education in *madrasas* outside the State, in Patna and Delhi. Shahid Ansari is a 25-year-old teacher in the NPS located in the Muslim hamlet. He left the local government school after class 4 and completed his matriculation from a *madrasa* in Patna, which was seen as more convenient and of better quality for his studies. 'My parents worried about my future if I only worked in the fields. Initially they sent me to the local school, but people used to tease me as I was older and we realised that it was better for me in an Urdu school'. He highlighted the role education plays in migration patterns from the village, especially for men:

> Many Santal and Muslim boys are leaving for schooling outside the village. They have the mission schools and we have the *madrasas*. Ours are government run and safe as well. There are a few close by, but it is better for the boys to go and live there, as they can study properly without distraction. My brother is now studying in a *madrasa* in Delhi. Nobody likes to send their children away, but the state of schools is so poor here, what will he stay here and do?

While success stories do exist, the numbers are small. Hardly one or two educated ST youth from the village have succeeded in securing regular, white-collar employment. Given the generally low quality of education, any educational success requires substantial additional investment, mainly in the form of private tutoring. Even if this is managed, the next hurdle comes in securing suitable jobs, those with long-term security, benefits and prospects. Almost all the educated STs in the village, though few in number, mentioned that merit was no longer an adequate criterion for securing a job – large amounts of money were required to pay bribes – and this they lacked.

What is clear is that there are many social dimensions of education which are seen as important both in terms of the experience of education and its contribution to distinction. The discipline, the teaching of English, the focus on studies to the exclusion of manual work – all these contribute to shaping values, lifestyles and people's sense of status and mobility. These markers, however, continue to be framed in relation to masculine identities and the task of provision. For both Hindu and Muslim girls, mobility can be acquired by marrying an educated man, preferably with regular employment. For the STs, where women equally participate with men in the workforce, girls too aspire for independent and socially valued careers. Here, however, the weight of mainstream social norms and cultural practices, reflected in school cultures and the high costs of private schooling, appear to be disadvantaging girls and leading to growing gender inequality.

Schooling as a gendered process

As visible from Table 2, the reorganisation of the schooling system in the village has most adversely affected ST girls. While there was a decline of 30 in the middle school, only 43 joined the new NPS. As mentioned earlier, there is no ST girl who has yet completed her matriculation from this village; at most they study up to the primary level. There are several ways of explaining this. First, ST boys themselves have not done too well, so despite the fact that there is no overt gender discrimination amongst the STs, in a general context of male dominance, girls are likely to face even stronger obstacles to success. Boys like Anil have gone in for contracting, but its very engagement with an essentially upper-caste, Hindu, male, public domain, makes it an area virtually impossible for ST girls, the exception perhaps could lie in the realm of contracting domestic workers.

The value of private/mission schooling for girls is, however, seen in the sphere of confidence-building, and for this five or six years of schooling are seen as sufficient. Kahan completed her primary education from the St James Mission School and was then married. Her in-laws were not good to her; she wanted to assert her independence, so ran away with a group of 10 girls to Delhi in April 2006:

> We were ill-treated by the placement agency, moved from one job to another, not paid a salary or given proper food. In three months, I realised I was pregnant, hence decided to come home – my schooling gave me the confidence to travel back alone. But when I returned, I discovered that my husband had taken another wife. I stayed with my parents till a satisfactory agreement was reached.

While schooling did not help her get a better job, or improve her working conditions, it did help gain confidence to negotiate with her husband and in-laws.

The other girls remained in Delhi, a few returned only in 2008, many of them with only a third of what was their due. None of the others had been to school; they did not know Hindi and could not travel on their own, without a woman from the agency accompanying them back. The agency retained some of their wage, this woman took her share, and they came home with very little. As Shanti said:

> I went due to poverty, so thought will earn and buy things for myself and my family. My mother was ill and I sent Rs 2000 home through the woman who took us, but she never gave them this money. I came home now after two years, but didn't get all my dues. I could not really argue for it.

While the access to and treatment in schools is one factor, part of the gender difference in educational attainment also arises from the gendered segmentation of the labour market. The 10 girls who migrated for domestic work from this village were all between the ages of 14 and 18, unlike a majority of migrant boys, often married and much older. The purpose for many of them was not to make a career in domestic work, rather to earn some money to relieve the poverty of their households, to accumulate a few personal assets or then to escape temporarily from excessive reproductive work burdens at home. As Sita said, 'I was doing so much work at home and was not appreciated at all. Everyone had their demands, so I decided to go to Delhi'. Their future lies in marriage and making a successful home, though this too may include temporary work migration on their own or along with their husbands. Sita has now migrated to the brick kilns along with her husband.

For Hindu girls, a few now completing secondary schooling, the purpose is not to seek jobs, rather to find a groom with a white-collar job. Educated men are perceived to have a preference for educated women to ensure performance of appropriate social roles as befits their status. With an increasing number of educated men, the demand for educated wives is also rising. As Sheila, the *balwadi* worker lamented, 'The day I got admission for pilot training was also the day that my marriage was arranged. What to do, I really wanted to work, but had to sacrifice my career, as marriage is seen as the most important event in a girl's life'.

Conclusions

In this paper I have explored the processes through which different forms of schooling are given value and meaning in their everyday use and practice. While higher education is positively associated with prospects for white-collar employment, which continues to be socially valued, there are no guarantees that this will in fact be the outcome of investment in education. This since the experience of education and its social practice continues to be mediated by personal characteristics of sex, age and ethnicity, as well as one's positioning within the existing class hierarchies. These are not inflexible, yet remain hard to penetrate for the socially disadvantaged such as the STs in a mixed-caste village.

Distinction is measured not just by the consumption of goods and services, in this case, education, but by the social trajectories of its acquisition and its social uses. It is this element that seems to provide the space for the exercise of agency and transforming existing hierarchies in social and gender relations. In this context, mission education appears to have an advantage over acquiring education in government schools or even *madrasas*. Apart from possibly better quality, the mission schools inculcate a set of norms and values, codes of conduct and discipline that conform to middle- and upper-class standards of distinction. Graduates of such schools may end up abhorring manual labour, and even while performing it, constantly seek other alternatives that help them maintain a particular lifestyle and image. This is not easy for the STs, evident from this village study, where barely a handful have escaped into other professions, as they are typically stereotyped as manual workers, with or without schooling.

For women, the picture has been mixed. While few have managed to complete secondary education or even aspire to white-collar jobs, even some basic schooling that provides elementary literacy and numeracy skills gives them a sense of personal confidence, enhancing their bargaining position, at least within their own households, if not with their employers. This is an important gain, as from a perspective of social mobility within the Indian context; this can be acquired not through women's employment, rather by restricting women to the role of good wives and mothers. And here too, mission education scores over state schooling, transmitting as it does notions of 'goodness' as seen in terms of discipline, obedience and quiet service, that can help women gain status within their marriages.

While the gains from education cannot be doubted, this paper has brought out the differences in educational choices and its social use for people positioned differently within existing social and gender hierarchies. Choice in fact operates at multiple levels: societal, parental and ultimately experienced by the child. The meaning and value attributed to schooling is not fixed, rather contingent on how individuals mediate and respond to lived experiences within existing structures of constraint. In fact, the very act of 'consuming' a particular type of schooling can lead to the acquisition of markers of distinction that can potentially contribute to social and economic mobility.

Acknowledgements
The research was carried out as part of a larger project on 'Gender Differences in Migration Opportunities: Implications for Educational Choices and Wellbeing Outcomes', funded by the Development Research Centre on Globalisation, Migration and Poverty, whose support is gratefully acknowledged. I would like to thank the villagers of Mahari, the teachers as well as the district and Block officials in Sahebgunj and Borio for their support, and the two anonymous *Compare* reviewers for constructive suggestions and comments.

Notes
1. Article 342, Part XVI of the Constitution of India provides for public notification by the President to specify the tribes that shall be deemed as Scheduled Tribes and hence eligible for special provisions to promote their educational and economic interests (Bakshi 1992). The historical disadvantage of the entire group was thus politically recognised.
2. Name of the village and people quoted have all been changed.
3. See http://education.nic.in/ssa/ssa_1.asp (accessed 24 October 2008).
4. One pound is approximately Rs 80.
5. Jeffrey, Jeffrey, and Jeffrey (2008: 583–4) note the importance of money, social contacts, then knowledge, in that order for securing government jobs.
6. These teachers are locally recruited, on fixed-wage contracts and not provided much training.
7. Rashtriya Swayamsevak Sangh (RSS) is a Hindu right-wing organisation, particularly hostile to missionaries and church groups in the state, seeing them as responsible for converting a large number of STs to Christianity, thus working against their cause of creating a Hindu nation.

References
Appadurai, A. 1996. *Modernity at large: Cultural dimensions of globalisation.* Minneapolis: University of Minnesota Press.
Assessment Survey Evaluation Research (ASER). 2007. *Annual status of education review.* New Delhi: Pratham.
Bakshi, P.M. 1992. *The constitution of India.* Delhi: Universal Book Traders.
Balagopalan, S. 2005. An ideal school and the schooled ideal: Education at the margins. In *Educational regimes in contemporary India,* ed. R. Chopra and P. Jeffery, 83–98. New Delhi: Sage Publications.
Bourdieu, P. 1984. *Distinction.* Cambridge, MA: Harvard University Press.
Bourdieu, P., and J.-C. Passeron. 1977. *Reproduction in education, society and culture.* London and Beverly Hills, CA: Sage.
Bowles, S., H. Gintis, and M.O. Groves, eds. 2005. *Unequal chances: Family background and economic success.* New York and Princeton, Russell Sage Foundation and Princeton University Press.
Bray, M. 2006. Private supplementary tutoring: Comparative perspectives on patterns and implications. *Compare* 36: 515–30.
Breman, J. 1985. *Of peasants, migrants and paupers: Rural labour circulation and capitalist production in West India.* New Delhi: Oxford University Press.
Caddell, M. 2006. Private schools as battlefields: Contesting visions of learning and livelihood in Nepal. *Compare* 36: 463–80.
Collins, J. 2009. Literacy as social reproduction and social transformation: The challenge of diasporic communities in the contemporary period. Plenary presentation, International Conference on Literacy Inequalities, September 1–3, in Norwich.

Erikson, R., and J.H. Goldthorp. 2002. Intergenerational inequality: A sociological perspective. *Journal of Economic Perspectives* 16, no. 3: 31–44.

Giroux, H.A. 1983. *Theory and resistance in education: A pedagogy for the opposition.* London: Heinemann Educational.

Government of India. 2001. *Census of India.* New Delhi: Registrar General of Census, Government of India.

Govinda, R., and M. Bandyopadhyay. 2007. *Access to elementary education in India: Country analytic review.* New Delhi: National University for Educational Planning and Administration.

Harma, J. 2009. Can choice promote Education for All? Evidence from growth in private primary schooling in India. *Compare* 39: 151–66.

Jackson, C., and N. Rao. 2009. Gender inequality and agrarian change in liberalizing India. In *The gendered impacts of liberalization,* ed. S. Razavi, 63–98. New York and London: Routledge.

Jeffrey, C., P. Jeffery, and R. Jeffery. 2008. *Degrees without freedom? Education, masculinities and unemployment in North India.* Stanford, CA: Stanford University Press.

Kumar, K. 1993. *What is worth teaching?* New Delhi: Orient Longman.

Longwe, S. 1998. Education for women's empowerment or schooling for women's subordination? *Gender and Development* 6, no. 2: 19–26.

Lynch, K. 1989. *The hidden curriculum: Reproduction in education, an appraisal.* London: The Falmer Press.

Mehrotra, S., and P.R. Panchamukhi. 2006. Private provision of elementary education in India: Findings of a survey in eight states. *Compare* 36: 421–42.

Miller, D., ed. 1995. *Acknowledging consumption: A review of new studies.* London and New York: Routledge.

Mosse, D., S. Gupta, M. Mehta, V. Shah, and J. Rees. 1999. Brokered livelihoods: Debt, labour migration and development in tribal Western India. *Journal of Development Studies* 38, no. 5: 59–88.

Nussbaum, M. 2000. *Women and human development: The capabilities approach.* New Delhi: Kali for Women.

PROBE Team. 1999. *Public report on basic education in India.* New Delhi: Oxford University Press.

Pryor, J. 2005. Can community participation mobilise social capital for improvement of rural schooling? A case study from Ghana. *Compare* 35: 193–204.

Rao, N. 2009. Migration, mobility and the assertion of masculinities in rural Bangladesh. Paper presented at the workshop on Learning, Livelihoods and Social Mobility, May 13–14, Brunel University.

Rose, P. 2009. Editorial introduction: Non-state provision of education – evidence from Africa and Asia. *Compare* 39: 127–34.

Sachar, R. 2007. *Report of the Commission on Social, Economic and Educational Status of the Muslim Community of India.* New Delhi: Akalank Publications.

Srivastava, P. 2006. Private schooling and mental models about girls' schooling in India. *Compare* 36: 497–514.

Subrahmanian, R. 2005. Education, exclusion and the development State. In *Educational regimes in contemporary India,* ed. R. Chopra and P. Jeffery, 62–82. New Delhi: Sage.

Tooley, J., and P. Dixon. 2006. 'De facto' privatisation of education and the poor: Implications of a study from sub-Saharan Africa and India. *Compare* 36: 443–62.

Unnithan-Kumar, M. 2003. Spirits of the womb: Migration, reproductive choice and healing in Rajasthan. *Contributions to Indian Sociology* 37, nos. 1–2: 163–88.

Willis, P. 1977. *Learning to labour: How working class kids get working class jobs.* Farnborough, UK: Saxon House, Teakfield.

'It is hard to stay in England': itineraries, routes, and dead ends: an (im)mobility study of nurses who became carers

Sondra Cuban

Educational Research, Lancaster University, Lancaster, UK

> This article presents findings from an Economic Social Research Council (ESRC) study on the roles of education in the trajectories of health care professionals who migrated to England and became carers. The study looks at the downward mobility and deskilling of these women, and their struggles to reverse their bungled career paths. The author maps the routes of women, who after receiving a nurse education in countries such as China, Malawi, Romania, Philippines, and India, attempt returns on their educational investments in England. The themes revealed that although these nurses developed ingenious strategies to advance their careers, many of them could not overcome the structural barriers that impeded their pathways to becoming health care professionals in a new country.

Introduction to the problem: nurse mobility through migration?

> Because I am working here as a senior care assistant, I haven't got any chance to work with my experience. (former nurse)

A picture on a Mills and Boon series cover of a 1987 doctor/nurse romance, *Nurse on the Move*, by Francis Crowne depicts a migrant British female nurse next to a German male doctor. The scene encapsulates the image of nurses using their careers for adventurous and social purposes. These illustrations are timeless and fixed in the popular imagination. This prerogative, two decades later, however, exists mainly for emigrating nurses from capital-rich countries rather than from developing ones. Nurses in the latter category often migrate because of few available options to practise their professions as well as other concerns related to poverty, as one woman explained: 'money talks ... we can earn a thousand pounds here [in England] in a month ... that's our one year's salary'. They see themselves as independent opportunists forging, 'a global treasure hunt for a better life' (Kingma 2006, 178).

Mary, for example, in a rural northwest region of England, and originally from Malawi, works long hours in a care home so as to advance herself and her children, as does Li-Mei, a nurse from China who is a care assistant (carer) at a nursing home. Both women have high hopes for their futures. Mary, for example, has decided she would like to become a doctor in England. She rationalized: 'when patients change conditions, I can't do anything about it. I call the doctor ... I want to be a doctor ... I have been in the background, and on the receiving end'. Li-Mei also wants to adapt her qualifications, so as to become a nurse again. These women, like other migrant nurses, saw care work as a stepping-stone towards health care professions in England. Yet both women had little support to advance and relied on their own strategies; Mary located access to medicine courses on the internet and after applying, received little feedback or information after she was rejected, while Li-Mei concluded that if she did not do anything about her situation she would never advance: 'I think if I stay in there [at the care home] I can't development my skill ... she [her manager] knows I'm a qualified nurse but she didn't help me. So I just want try myself'.

This case study captures the downward pressures (Walters 2000) in migrant nurses' 'race to the bottom', in an era of market-based health care reforms and profit-based qualifications industries that require huge investments from individual women. Although migrant nurses may begin their careers as, 'nurses on the move' (Kingma 2006) (symbolising the promise of social mobility), they too often become 'nurses on the ropes' (Gordon 2005, 274) in their search for a better life, and eventually become deskilled in a political economy of care, which utilizes their skills without giving them credit (Yeates 2005). While their capacity to advance in spite of such oppressive conditions is evident, I highlight the forces that shape the trajectories of 23 health care professionals (mostly nurses) who were senior carers and carers in England and their lived experiences of labour and (im)mobility. The study addresses questions of why so many migrant health care professionals become deskilled and how they deal with their situations. In this article I explore the literature on nurse migration and the ways migrant nurses slide into positions of servitude as care assistants (carers) (Anderson 2000). Then I offer a background on nurse education across developing and advanced countries. Next I describe the methodology, including interviews with nurses about their education and migration experiences, and the various barriers they faced to advancement. To conclude, I offer policy implications surrounding women, migration, and education.

Literature review: transnational flows of gendered skilled labour

Having moved from the knowledge economy (of nursing) to the secondary service sector (as carers), nurses, like Mary and Li-Mei, were unable to transfer their educational capital to a meaningful currency in a new country. Due to the lack of international standards and the complexities of adaptation, as well as other factors that will be explored, migrant nurses often circulate on a 'carousel' of low-skilled positions; in spite of their persistence, they are unable to get their promised job (Kingma 2006). Therefore, Mary and Li-Mei's stories would not be in a Mills and Boon series described above. Both women felt trapped within a 'chain' of global care in a market that had been vacated by locals and neglected by a neo-liberal government focused on privatizing welfare and depending on them to solve the crisis (Brush and Vasupurum 2006). This 'global care chain' (Ehrenreich and Hochschild 2002) kept them enclosed in a cycle of being persistently 'dislocated' (Parrenas 2001) in jobs that enabled them to survive, but with little time or energy to connect to better opportunities; whilst 70% of all Filipino carers and 50% of those carers from Africa have tertiary education, only 30% of all British-born carers do (Haour-Knipe and Davies 2008). Consider another nurse-turned-carer, Manny, who was in her mid-thirties, and from the Philippines with three children. Her story mocks the romance genre for the ways she used an online dating service to find a partner who might sponsor her and her family. Entering England on a student visa, and, in knowing that she had limited time before it expired, she invested all of her energies in this venture, explaining: 'I am Filipina and I want to bring my children here. I put my real life on [this service] and I said I am separated and have three kids and they (two men in their forties and sixties) are interested in me and I give them a chance. The reason is because *it is hard to stay in England*'. Furthermore, carers like Manny became even more dependent on 'helpers' (paid domestic workers and care workers) as well as other family members to care for their children, incurring demands on them from both ends in terms of surviving in a pricey environment while remitting enough money to raise the quality of life for their families.

Recruiting female skilled migrant labour for care work has been a primary strategy for the new global care industry, who brand them as heroes holding up advanced and developing countries (Kofman and Raghuram 2006). While policy makers view this group as 'aspiring' they pay little attention to the barriers blocking their way and carers are blamed for not 'integrating' (Raghuram 2007). 'Aspiring migrants' are defined in opportunistic terms by government agencies:

> They take on low-skilled or unskilled roles while they improve their English or gain a relevant qualification to allow them to practise their profession. An aspiring migrant could be a medical doctor working as a labourer at a building site, or a graduate at the beginning of their work career. *Aspiring migrants are happy to make easy money doing unskilled work and view it in the context of being an opening to greater opportunities.*
> (Learning and Skills Council 2006, 24–5)

This viewpoint begs the question as to whether 'aspiring migrants' are truly 'happy' to take on this burden; whether there are genuine opportunities that are awaiting them and if they are able to advance at the same time they are being deskilled. From the experiences of Mary, Manny and Li-Mei, it would seem that the quagmire of qualifications actually stall their mobility by mandating low-paid work as the above quote attests. There are few means for transferring qualifications in spite of nursing shortages and social care employers are able to recruit health care professionals on the cheap. Still nurses aspire because, as one woman in this study expresses: 'I wish to be working like a nurse – *it's my job*'. The definition of aspiring neglects institutional barriers, such as the inability for migrants to apply their professional skills and knowledge because of limited adaptation and education opportunities, not to mention restrictive immigration legislation, especially for third country migrants (those from non-EU countries), few social protections, in addition to sexism and racism within the nursing profession and gender polarization in care markets (Kenway and Kelly 2000; Winkleman-Gleed 2006). Another nurse-turned-carer in this study, Anna, said: 'Another reason for migrating [to England] is experience. I want to go to Canada ... because its very expensive to stay here in England'.

This issue is critical for *women* in particular. The most popular route, since the 1990s, for skilled women to migrate has been through the nursing profession. While Britain has historically 'poached' nurses from developing countries, especially the West Indies, since the 1950s, the beginning of the twenty-first century represents the most extensive recruitment campaign in years (McNeil-Walsh 2004) because of a reduced amount of opportunities to practise in their own countries and welfare reform in England: 'Skilled women migrants are precisely being enticed to migrate in order to provide welfare' (Raghuram and Kofman 2006, 3). An in-depth study of migrant nurses from Kerala, India showed that nursing schools sprang up as a 'passport to go abroad' and existed to 'financially save the house' (George 2005, 53). One nurse in this study stated, 'Nursing has become a business ... if they build a hospital, its main source of income is the nursing school they attach to it' (George 2005, 53). These schools charge a lot of money and short-staffed hospitals depend on recently graduated nurses to volunteer in them because they cannot often afford to pay them wages. Nurses often want to migrate to earn a decent living and arrive in England only to fulfil a carer shortage. While many nurses bank their own and their family investments with agents who promise them eventual nursing posts in well-paying hospitals in England, many of them end up in private nursing homes or agencies, caring for the elderly, which has become a new migrant ghetto and contributes to brain waste (Kingma 2006). Anna, explained: 'I have training as a nurse and graduated as nurse, but we are here. We forgot something. We are not updated and we miss the hospital setting. It sometimes happens that there is an emergency, but we can't apply our experience'.

As the social care industry is increasingly becoming occupationally specific, it is also demanding more labour from workers, including everything from paperwork to cleaning – turning these carers into 'maids on the move' (Momsen 1999). As Anderson (2000) found, in her study of domestic work, the lines between care and cleaning activities were hard to draw because it was so inclusive that the definition of care became blurry. Using a list by the International Labour Organisation for domestic work occupations, she shows that personal care is omitted, which contradicted what the domestic workers in her study said they did on the job. On the other end, Sterland and Talbott-Strettle (2007) studied Polish carers in England (most of whom were former nurses in Poland) and found that their actual caring consisted of a heavy amount of domestic work with general cleaning, washing clothes and curtains, ironing, cleaning windows, dusting, vacuuming, collecting linens and making beds, and cleaning wheelchairs near the top of their list of daily work. Studies of health care work describe the occupation in ways that suggest that carers are supposed to take on increasing amounts of work *and* education, including, training classes, qualifications, and paperwork, that includes an inexhaustible list of skills and technologies (Brown and Kirpal 2005) so that nurses do not have to be 'caught at the level of the patient' (Thorne 2006). This switch is significant, in a profession (nursing) that has promoted scientific management so that it can be 'a marketable commodity' (Jarvis 1997, 29; Yorks and Sharoff 2001). With new qualifications that are mandated under the 2000 Care Standards Act, care agencies who train their already skilled migrant workers can advertise themselves as offering more 'professional' and low-priced services by 'quasi-nurses' (Hauor-Knipe and Davies 2008).

Background on global nurse migration and the role of education

Education and migration are inextricably connected, as 'no nurse can move either internally or externally if she does not have the proper education' (Kingma 2006, 81). Kingma's context (2006) for global nursing education and migration is advantageous for highlighting the trajectories of a group of nurse/carers in England and the structural forces that both push and pull them. She sketches three major steps in migrant nurses' career pathways that involve education: (1) acquiring a professional education (itineraries for their careers); (2) adapting and obtaining a foreign licence through certifying qualifications or taking courses on nursing (routes toward a new career in a new country); and (3) acquiring visas and work permits by employers through new immigration rules (dead ends when they become trapped as carers or in jobs with low salaries). The following metaphors were modified to illuminate these steps: the first one, 'itineraries' indicates the professional trajectories of migrant health care professionals. These are linked to the second one – their maps for travelling abroad to become practitioners in a new country, which can be called: 'routes'. Then, when they settle into their jobs in ways that send them into downward cycles or stagnation, the metaphor 'dead ends' captures this syndrome.

Step 1: getting an education becomes an itinerary to go abroad

The itineraries of migrant nurses are first developed in nursing schools, with financial costs as the main factor for their enrollment (to the nursing student and her family). The costs are so overwhelming in developing countries that they can quickly determine nurses' migration decisions and plans. These schools are central actors in nurse migration, with the purpose to export nurses; a common promotional slogan is, 'your cap is your passport' (Kingma 2006, 23). Yet England also plays a strong role in this 'education export industry' (Kingma 2006, 9); one of the main reasons given for the nursing shortage in the England is the closure of nursing schools and the downsizing of nurse education institutions since the 1980s. It is cheaper for English hospitals to receive a migrant nurse from a developing country than to train one (Kingma 2006, 192). They may join with other countries to offer nursing school education, which adds to confusion over standards. Governments in transitional/developing countries are more reluctant to fund nursing schools especially if students leave and never return (and compensations are not enforced). This brain drain phenomenon forces individual women to pay a lot of money for their education, making nursing 'one of the expensive careers for girls to take and a most profitable one for the hospital owners [who depend on newly minted nurses to volunteer in them] ... since they spend so much for their education, naturally their tendency after graduation is to go abroad' (Kingma 2006, 85).

Step 2: the routes to nursing get blocked because of adaptation barriers

Every migrant nurse needs to figure out a route towards becoming a nurse in England. The adaptation process is complicated by a number of factors, including uneven assessment procedures and policies in the profession, ethnocentric language regulations as well as accumulating costs, university accreditation problems, lack of mentors, little access to programmes, and lack of information that can obstruct the pathway towards becoming licensed. Each nation determines its own regulations, preparation and qualifications and the process itself is highly bureaucratic and governed by many different regulatory bodies. This licensing route is described as a 'superhighway', making migrant nurses pay tolls along the way towards being a practitioner (Kingma 2006, 95). Before and after she completes her adaptation, large amounts of paperwork are gathered to determine the credibility of her qualifications, which can be difficult if translations are required. England's system often demands that non-EU students take prerequisite courses and pre-tests, which also cost money, and are income-generators for the industry. In England, the Nurse Midwifery Council (NMC) uses the International English Language Test System (IELTS) exam, which is required for third country migrants (non-EU citizens), before being able to become a qualified nurse. Each test costs around £100, with a minimum score of 7 needed (raised from 6.5 in 2007); another monetary barrier is created, especially for retakes. Nationality is a major barrier over and beyond language; for example, Filipinas who studied nursing for four years in English have to take this test rather than a Polish nurse, who is an EU citizen, but who might have much less oral and written fluency in English.

Step 3: visas and work regulations lead to dead ends in nursing homes

Neither a nursing school education nor a foreign licence guarantees that a nurse will be able to practise in England if she does not have the right visa and work regulation. Immigration policies are critical for whether or not a nurse can get a job. Legislation criteria can fluctuate wildly, and link to skills gap occupations, and points-based systems, privileging some nationalities over others, and leading recruitment agencies to find loopholes and charge twice. The build up of pressures at this point may make the migrant nurse/carer feel like she has hit a dead end, especially when she invests a great deal of money (thousands of dollars or pounds), and cannot locate a well-paid job in a hospital. One major problem is the accrual of debts that make the nurse beholden to banks, agencies, distant relatives, employers, in addition to her own network of colleagues and peers. Once nurses arrive at their destination, they have to rely on a number of spin-off services to connect to their homes, including long-distance calling and remittances services, which is also a major source of income for developing and advanced economies (Phillips 2009). If a nurse comes through an overseas agency, she may pay for the initial fee and contacts, or have money returned to the agency as part of her salary (Kingma 2006, 111).

Kingma (2006) has argued that nurses do not protest because they lack access to information about unions, have previous negative experiences of making complaints, and do not want to rock the boat in a new job and in a new country. At the same time, professional organizations do not want to be involved with 'migrant nurses' problems' because they see these issues as 'social' not professional; the perception is that migrant nurse recruitment lowers salaries for all nurses. Subsequently, many migrant nurses end up in poorly paid privately owned care homes or nursing homes. Restrictive immigration legislation has also made it possible for nursing homes to recruit nurses but to hire them as senior carers on contracts that make it difficult for them to leave.

Overview

Kingma's background on the professional processes and outcomes of migrant nurses is important for understanding the complex ways that education operates as both an affordance and an obstacle in their mobility. While institutional barriers are rife in Kingma's conceptualization, what is not discussed are the strategies that these migrants deploy to cope with these forces. This study forges a path between structure and agency to see how they operate together for migrant nurses in England and their advancement pathways.

The study methodology

This exploratory study 'grounds' the experiences and perspectives of women migrant nurses in local and global contexts, using the research to build themes about this transnational phenomenon. Interviews with 23 migrant women, from two data sets, who were former health care professionals but were currently operating as carers and recent nurses in private care homes and nursing homes in England took place between 2007 and 2009. The interviews focused on the reasons why the nurses migrated, the steps they took to come to England, their previous work and education in their country of origin, and elsewhere, as well as how they continued to learn and obtain educational opportunities and the barriers they faced to advancement. Observations of 16 of the women in their workplaces and, in some cases, at home were also made in addition to training and education courses they attended, so as to balance out what they said with what they did. Photographs were also taken of the women at work; a secreted world that is rarely captured visually yielded important background information to complement the field notes. These data were analysed through Grounded Theory so as to see patterns of the nurses in advancing their careers (Strauss and Corbin 1997). Due to the reductiveness and decontextualization of Grounded Theory in its search for general patterns, case studies of 10 carers were developed to highlight their voices and reveal close-up social changes. Furthermore, a Delphi study of 60 experts in the fields of immigration, nursing, care, unions, and the field of English for Speakers of Other Languages (ESOL) was conducted so as to link national and international issues and which allowed for a holistic view of the problem.

About the women health care professionals

Six Filipinas were nurses, while two were occupational therapists. Three of them who were recent nurse graduates were on student visas, while the rest were on regular work visas that had various levels of complications due to their status. All but two had children, some of whom were also in England. There were four Romanians, three of whom had children and families working in the care homes in the study. While three of them became nurses again, the process took them two years each and they worked in nursing homes, earning slightly over their former care worker salaries and some operated as carers too. Of the nine Indian (mainly Keralan) nurses, seven were married and mothers of young children and one was a nurse educator. Only two became nurses during the interview period. Other participants were a Malawian widow who was a nurse with three children in England, and a Chinese single nurse. Of these health care professionals, only a third of them were senior carers. Their ages varied, with the average being in their early thirties. The next section presents the women's strategies for mobility and themes of immobility (Urry 2007).

Strategies for mobility and themes of (im)mobility

All of the women had problematic situations that confirmed the literature and Kingma's schema. They also presented issues that went beyond these conceptualizations, which suggested further enquiry and more attention to their advancement strategies. The women's ability to access education and advance were fraught with difficulties related to their employers, immigration status, the recruitment agencies, discrimination, and work conditions. The women were segregated into privately owned care home companies, rather than in the public National Health Service (NHS) hospital system, which precipitated difficulties in adapting and acquiring information about career opportunities. There were few established networks and support systems for them that could have scaffolded them into better positions in the nursing market. Furthermore, immigration systems for non-EU and EU members played important roles in advancement. Yet they continued to press for more opportunities.

Getting an education: costly itineraries

Many women said they dreamt of becoming nurses, and saw nursing school as a 'privilege'. One woman said: 'I had this opportunity to be a nurse, to be able to work in a hospital so I took a nursing course. Yeah, I had a *privilege* to work in a hospital because when I was a little girl I was dreaming to be a nurse'. Others pushed their sisters into nursing for similar reasons, like one who said: 'I pushed my sister to go for nursing, 'it is good for you, you will get a good job and a good career, and you'll get a good experience'. While families were important in shaping careers, the women could defy them, as one carer articulated: 'I always wanted to be a nurse, [but] my parents wanted me to be a teacher so I got a certificate and obeyed them and went to college. After college I used my professional credentials to get an appointment at a hospital and develop a nursing career'. Some of the women attended university hospitals that were far from where they lived. Attending reputable urban universities awarded them status in the profession and opened doors for them to get jobs abroad as a step up the nursing ladder. especially in the Middle East where several of them worked before coming to England. The nurses also discussed what they learnt from their specialties, like one who recollected: 'I moved from a rural area to a city, New Delhi, which had the highest rating and I worked with critical cases there for nine months. I was a specialist in a hospital for one year and three months. I did in-service training one year abroad. It was a dream of some of my friends to go and I was selected and went to Riyadh'.

For most of the women, however, nursing school was reported as being laborious and it was difficult for them to differentiate their schooling from their working hours. The long working hours on wards in hospitals, in conjunction with low or no wages and staff shortages during their internship (in-service) period, and upon graduating, drew the most negative comments, and appeared to be strong push factors for them to migrate. One nurse said, 'I am a nurse, in a government hospital for five years. We work really hard, 50–60 patients in a ward. Not paid well'. They knew there were better opportunities elsewhere and searched high and low, like another nurse who said: 'In India, there is no salary and opportunity ... I searched for a job in India for a month'. Push factors were related to access to technologies: 'I like to work abroad', one nurse said, 'and I want to study more about here because here there is more advanced technologies and everything so I had to work with these old technologies which is why I came here'. The women also took additional English-language tests to prepare themselves for nursing abroad even thought they used English in nursing school, like one nurse exclaimed: 'Teaching in nurse school is in English and we have to speak English!' This fact made it difficult for many of them to accept that recipient countries demanded English-language tests from them, to be considered acceptable. Similar to what Hauor-Knipe and Davies (2008) found in their study, these carers considered the system to be arbitrary and exclusive.

Nearly all of the women migrated through recruitment agencies, which, upon collecting all of their paperwork and fees, promised the women that they would earn easy money as carers while they adapted as nurses. Yet most of them did not know the meaning of being a 'carer' with one describing her position as a 'nanny'. Nor did they understand the difficulties surrounding adaptation. Another carer who understood that the work she did was considered to be low-skilled by British standards, rationalized that the employers and recruiters wanted the paperwork as insurance of the employees' characters.

Adaptation and licences: routes in limbo

After non-EU nurses arrived in England, a number of them started adaptation courses through their own savings and bank and family loans and gifts, with the assumption that they would become nurses and remit. While they went through their course work, they had to wait to finish their programmes because of bureaucratic delays at their universities. If they had student visas, they were required to take additional courses, even if they were remotely related to nursing, for which the universities profited. The new adaptation graduates waited for their nursing licences (pin numbers) after they completed their courses or if they were EU members (who did not need to take adaptation courses), they waited for their translated degrees to be accepted and were applying for nursing positions. All of them were biding their time as carers while they waited for the process to finish. Often they might call their families every day for support because they were depressed about having to wait and waste additional money. One woman said: 'That's the main difference I feel from India and England, the cost of living is very, very high here. I am earning the money but the thing is ... I am getting the money and the same time going [out]. Expenses, daily expenses, it's much'.

Anyone in the process of adapting had to join the NMC. In order to join it, if they were not from the EU, they had to take the IELTS and pass it with a high score that had recently been raised in 2007. Despite English-language nursing education in the Philippines and India, many of them took additional English-language courses to increase their marketing potential. They studied for this test on their own time, in colleges, and with books from the library. This test posed several problems for the women, and caused anxiety since a certain score was needed. One woman who failed it was disappointed as she was a nurse educator in India and used English to teach her students. She said:

> I took the IELTS and got 6 points less ... I want to take that test again. Took it at the agency. I approached them and they said go as a senior carer to England, take the test in Manchester and get adaptation. In India there are many places to learn English though. I paid the agency £600. My parents gave me the money ... I was disappointed I was a carer, not a nurse but the agency explained everything, if you want to do the test. I still felt disappointed.

Another carer who received a score of 6 in India and had no time to retake it before her NMC registration period was over, exclaimed: 'I will be unlucky to do the adaptation here – I lost my good chance'. While she engaged in National Vocational Qualifications (NVQ) training because it was mandated for carers, she recognized that the NVQs were questionable on the nursing market. She said: 'Because I don't need to do the NVQ because my nursing side of it is equal to the NVQ3 ... the manager said I needed the certificate of NVQ3'.

Those nurses who entered on student visas were required to work as carers and take the NVQ3 for thousands of pounds through private training companies even if their company offered it for free. Three of the carers enrolled in a bogus training agency through their recruitment agencies. This registered training agency had a reputation for unscrupulous activities but continued to take in more students. When the training agency folded, the agency staff wrongly accused the carers of not paying fees and threatened to report them to the UK Border Agency, thereby leaving them vulnerable to deportation. None of the carers were able to get refunds, even after an investigation found the agency owners to be in the wrong. One carer described her situation:

> I hold a student visa. We have been paying tuition fees to the training centre, but no assessor, no training materials given. I tried ringing them and to get in touch but it's only an answering machine. The training centre closed down and we are going to be in trouble if we don't find a [new] training centre because of the UK Border Agency.

These students had to re-enroll in colleges and other training companies for additional monies to complete their NVQs, with the average fee being approximately £1500 for a course.

Visas and work permits: unlucky dead ends

Many overseas recruitment agencies charged both the employers and their recruits. The women paid different fees, which did not appear to be based on any standard – while some paid a few hundred British pounds, others paid thousands of pounds, particularly students and those from outside the EU. Two of the carers, for example, from the Philippines, paid nearly £9000. Often they were told that the paperwork was the main reason for their fees and a few of them were told to give cash with no receipts and to 'trust' them. One woman who paid too much money to an agency was soon abandoned without a place to work once she arrived in England. She recounted:

> I was unlucky. I tried to speak to the owner but couldn't get through because the owner of the agency is in the US. The nursing home didn't accept me, as it was a new manager and said they'd stop hiring ... The owner moved to the US and couldn't locate her. I reported her at immigration, and I wasted my phone cards. I don't have a receipt. 'You need to trust me', she said. The agreement was, 'you trust me, 50/50'.

None of the nurses, including new EU members, seemed to know that they could have identified a care home online, and go to a regulated and reputable recruitment agency in England to oversee their employment for less money.

Many of the nurses on work permits were worried about being able to stay in their current positions or feared they could not get new ones in a political climate that had become increasingly hostile to international staff. New legislation to limit visa renewals and length of extensions and contracts were considerable factors in the nurses becoming employed and extending visas. Additionally, employers who were nervous about the legislation were not applying for permits, thereby limiting the pool of available jobs. Many of the women with children abroad wondered how they would sponsor them into England with such wildly fluctuating legislation that made their futures so unpredictable.

Housing costs were a problem in terms of the rental prices, as well as utilities, council tax and TV licences, and broadband/wifi. Most of the women, although they were earning more money in England, felt shocked at the high expenses, which caused tensions around remitting, with a few of them depending on reverse remittances from families abroad to cope with the cost of living; one carer could not afford basic necessities and counted on family members in Germany to send food and clothes. Finally, a number of the women mentioned discriminatory experiences at work, which they did not report because they were worried about their immigration status and their abilities to progress as nurses. One carer remembered a client who yelled, 'fatty fatty Indian I don't like you. I will call the management and you will be reported next week'. While five of the carers did adapt, four of them worked in nursing homes earning approximately £10 an hour which is less than most NHS nurses' salaries. Their rotas were often overloaded too. One nurse, in saying she felt like, 'starting over as new' decided to work doubly hard to prove herself as a worthy adapted nurse, and in doing so, ended up in hospital with exhaustion and illnesses. She said: 'I'm getting £10.14 an hour – it's a 36 hours a week contract ... I'm working 50 hours a week, more than that maybe'.

Policy implications: rewarding enterprising identities

While the nurses followed all of the set pathways for obtaining an education or training in order to fulfil their aspirations of becoming health care professionals in their countries of origin and many of them attempted it in England, their efforts were risky. Most nurses were disappointed in their predicaments and were ambivalent about whether they had made the right decision to migrate to expand their career options with such great sacrifices. Several nurses did indeed adapt. For those who did adapt and became nurses, most ended up working in private nursing homes with minor salary increases.

The carers felt that they were not building or expanding on their previous skills and knowledge, and were not being upskilled beyond very basic means – often calling themselves 'unlucky'. They had little information about where to go to seek out advancement opportunities and relied exclusively on their small collegial networks, which served the purpose of helping them to survive in their current jobs rather than networking them to better ones. They also had little wherewithal or information about how to protest their situations on a formal level, and attempted to deal with their problems as individuals rather than in an organized way.

The training that they were offered in their workplaces (NVQs) did not translate to higher credentials or opportunities and were essentially unmarketable in the nursing industry. Still, the women withstood the obstacles they faced and thought they could overcome them by becoming more enterprising in their own efforts (and without formal supports). They used their limited resources ingeniously to gain advantages wherever they could; in spite of the labour-intensive effort and cost of the adaptation courses, a number of the women attempted it, and several of them did become nurses. But this was far from the majority (only five, and three were EU citizens), and the minority's successes came at considerable costs – emotional, financial, physical, professional, and otherwise: their enterprising activities were little rewarded. Furthermore, two of the five nurses who adapted worked for the same company, alternating at times, as both carers and nurses.

It is critical to look at women's higher education and their engagement in the care professions through labour *and* education markets rather than one or the other. Gender and race regimes (see also Rao 2010, in this issue) appear to play a significant role in these nurses' take up of the gender contract and their treatment in the care industry. Women care professionals are becoming increasingly monitored in a global economy focused on de-regulation (outsourced care companies) and re-regulation of the workplace (the establishment of Care Standards). In addition, as more women's occupations become restructured within the knowledge industries, such as nursing, where upskilling becomes mandatory, employers have not responded to their greater proficiencies and allowed for their autonomy and upward mobility (Walby 2002). While regulation in England has increased in the care sector to reassure the public that the elderly's care is professionalized, and standards are met, it does not appear to benefit migrant nurses who are already trained, but whose previous qualifications are considered illegitimate. With the 1990s expansion of markets in conjunction with health care reform, more studies became available especially on skilled women's trajectories (Kofman and Raghuram 2006). Yet these gender-based studies were overlooked by migration experts who focus principally on the IT and finance sectors which are known for being predominantly male, leaving the impression that everyone with a higher education who migrates is in a similar boat (Kofman and Raghuram 2004). This picture neglects the work of skilled women in the global care economy, namely social work, health, and education fields (often referred to as the 'semi-professions') where individual returns on educational investments are fewer (Carnoy 2005). Even while higher education in developing countries has increased for women, it also creates a supply of workers with fewer opportunities, other than to enter the international care market, further stimulating migration (Phillips 2009).

In this study, and as the literature notes, few sponsors (in education sectors, business or government bodies) paved the way from and to the workplace to higher education circuits that could genuinely advance these migrant care workers. While 'third mission' universities and colleges (Nedeva 2008) take on for-profit sectors, the international students and workers who are recruited get neglected. Under neo-liberal pushes, universities and businesses are increasingly bedfellows in offering adaptation, trainings such as the NVQ, and prerequisite nursing courses in order to feather their nests. This leads to the question of whether or not professional education in the care fields (such as nursing) offers serious advancement strategies for women if their credentials are constantly needing upgrading and shifting standards make their education invisible in destination countries: are women progressing at all in the global marketplace when they end up in lower-paying service positions? In assessing women's progress in education, European systems of measurement count women's participation in education and training, but neglect the 'segregation of women in areas of education that lead to less well-paid jobs' (Walby 2002, 381).

The commodification of care in labour markets and education and training appear to be intertwined with gender regimes. The transnational processes of women migrant nurses attempting to advance in a knowledge economy dominated by multinational firms (Stromquist 2002) which use education and training as a means of maximizing profits, reflect the symbiotic relationships of welfare reform within a global economy and the disadvantages of globalization on some professional women's trajectories and aspirations. This study points to the rise of the migration industry in the late 2000s (recruitment agencies with training companies and colleges and universities as well as testing agencies) in colluding with the government to stall the advancement of qualified care professionals by determining salaries, contract length, subjects of study, all of which can lead to unethical recruitment and brain waste.

The complex interplay of markets, described above, makes it difficult to find easy solutions for overturning the systematic deskilling of women health care professionals, especially because the policies are heavily responsible for this situation. Innovative reforms to support these women are needed on top levels. A good starting place would be to incorporate this population in to gender mainstreaming movements. This would involve unions (perhaps through the International Labour Organisation and Public Services International which campaigns for migrant women health care workers) reaching out, in conjunction with ethnic and professional associations, university advocate groups, as well as feminist organizations to create leadership opportunities for this group and to spread information across borders to counter exploitative recruitment and training agencies, bogus university and college programmes, and discriminatory employment and recruitment practices. Informal interventions can occur in ESOL, IELTS, adaptation, and social care foundation courses, and in student support services, as well as in printed materials (such as *Gender and Migration News*). Introduced at the Fourth World Conference on Women in Beijing in 1995, gender mainstreaming allows for gender-based budgeting, assessments, and the tools to assess women's capabilities in the system as well as concrete outcomes for women's development in the labour market (Walby 2005). Skilled migrant women in the developing world should be included in these initiatives.

To conclude, this study raises questions about the degree to which education and skills operate as levers and barriers in migrant health care professional women's abilities to advance. The argument for giving special consideration to this group and their needs for advancement can be made, especially if these former nurses, even in a temporary capacity, apply their expertise to their care work and raise its status and quality; through their care ethic and practices, they transform social care from the ground up, rather than through policy dictates. While these workers, with higher education, as well as non-migrant workers, who are well-trained, can lend the care industry a more esteemed image (as 'professional'), higher education and training, in and of themselves, do not necessarily empower women and should not be the main criteria in improving the sector.

Returning to romantic notions of care inscribed on the Mills and Boon series cover, a sober and systematic approach is needed to overturn the ways gender operates as an occupational determinant, how care is constructed in downwardly mobile ways for most of its female workforce, and the invisibility of prior learning and knowledge of health care professionals. Moreover, the ways the government Border Agency exploits the labour of skilled women through its points-based system needs to be protested. Breaking the silence may be the first step towards reversing systems that use skilled migrant women labour to construct discriminatory care regimes.

References

Anderson, B. 2000. *Doing the dirty work? The global politics of domestic labour*. New York: Zed Books.

Brown, A., and S. Kirpal. 2003. 'Old nurses with new qualifications are best'. In *Skills that matter,* ed. C. Warhurst, E. Keep, and I. Grugulis, 225–42. New York: Palgrave.

Brush, B.L., and R. Vasupuram. 2006. Nurses, nannies and caring work: Importation, visibility, and marketability. *Nursing Inquiry* 13, no. 3: 181–5.

Carnoy, M. 2005. Globalization, educational trends and the open society. Paper presented at the OSI Education conference 'A Critical Look at New Perspectives and Demands'. http:/

/www.international.ac.uk/resources/Open%20society%Institute.pdf (accessed January 16, 2010).

Ehrenreich, B., and A.R. Hochschild. 2002. *Global women: Nannies, maids, and sex workers in the new economy.* New York: Metropolitan Books.

George, S. 2005. *When women come first: Gender and class in transnational migration.* Berkeley: University of California Press.

Gordon, S. 2005. *Nursing against the odds: How health care cost cutting, media stereotypes and medical hubris undermine nurses and patient care.* Ithaca, NY: Cornell University Press.

Haour-Knipe, M., and A. Davies. 2008. *Return migration of nurses.* Geneva: International Centre for Nurse Migration.

Jarvis, P. 1997. The globalization of nurse education within higher education. *Nurse Education Today* 17: 23–30.

Kenway, J., and P. Kelly. 2000. Local/global markets and the restructuring of gender, schooling, and work. In *Globalization and education,* ed. N. Stromquist and K. Monkman, 173–97. Lanham, MD: Rowman & Littlefield.

Kingma, M. 2006. *Nurses on the move: Migration and the global health care economy.* Ithaca, NY: ILR Press.

Kofman, E., and P. Raghuram. 2006. Gender and global labour migrations: Incorporating skilled workers. *Antipode* 38: 282–303.

Learning and Skills Council. 2006. *Migrant workers and the labour market.* Coventry: Learning and Skills Council.

McNeil-Walsh, C. 2004. Widening the discourse: A case for the use of post-colonial theory in the analysis of South African nurse migration to Britain. *Feminist Review* 77: 120–4.

Momsen, J.H. 1999. *Gender, migration, and domestic service.* London: Routledge.

Nedeva, M. 2008. New tricks and old dogs: The 'third mission' and the re-production of the university. In *The world yearbook of education 2008: Geographies of knowledge/ geometries of power – higher education in the 21st century,* ed. D. Epstein, R. Boden, R. Deem, F. Rizvi, and S. Wright, 85–104. Routledge: New York.

Parrenas, R. 2001. *Servants of globalization: Women, migration, and domestic work.* Stanford, CA: Stanford University Press.

Phillips, N. 2009. Migration as development strategy? The new political economy of disposession and inequality in the Americas. *Review of International Political Economy* 16, no. 2: 231–59.

Raghuram, P. 2007. Interrogating the language of integration: The case of internationally recruited nurses. *Journal of Critical Nursing* 16: 2246–51.

Raghuram, P., and E. Kofman. 2006. Out of Asia: Skilling, reskilling, and deskilling of female migrants. *Women Studies International Forum* 27: 95–100.

Rao, N. 2010. Aspiring for distinction: Gendered educational choices in an Indian village. *Compare* 40: 000–000.

Sterland, L., and L. Talbott-Strettle 2007. *Skills for care: Polish migrant workers skills audit report.* Leicester: NIACE

Stromquist, N.P. 2002. Globalization, the I, and the Other. *Current Issues in Comparative Education* 4, no. 2: 87–94.

Strauss, A., and J. Corbin. 1997. *Grounded theory in practice.* London: Sage.

Thorne, S.E. 2006. Nursing education: Key issues for the 21st century. *Nurse Education Today* 26: 614–21.

Urry, J. 2007. *Mobilities.* Cambridge: Polity.

Walby, S. 2002. Gender and the economy: Regulation or deregulation? Paper for the ESRC seminar 'Work, Life and the New Economy', October, in Lancaster.

Walby, S. 2005. *Measuring women's progress in a global era.* Oxford: UNESCO.

Walters, S. 2000. Globalization, adult education, and development. In *Globalization and education,* ed. N.P. Stromquist and K. Monkman. Lanham, 197–218. MD: Rowman & Littlefield Publishers.

Winkelman-Gleed, A. 2006. *Migrant nurses, motivation, integration, contribution.* Oxford: Radcliffe Medical Press.

Yeates, N. 2005. A global political economy of care. *Social Policy & Society* 4: 227–34.

Yorks, L., and L. Sharoff. 2001. An extended epistemology for fostering transformative learning in holistic nursing education. *Holistic Nursing Practice* 16, no. 1: 21–9.

To fairly tell: social mobility, life histories, and the anthropologist

Véronique Benei

Centre National de la Recherche Scientifique (LAIOS/IIAC), Paris, France and *London School of Economics, London, UK*

> This article focuses on social agents' own understandings of socio-economic mobility and social achievement, exploring the possibilities offered by the tool of *family* life history in the context of formerly Untouchable communities in western India, Maharashtra. While arguing in favour of family life histories as both resource and method in the Indian context, I reconsider the positivist functionalist stance dominant in studies of social mobility until the last decade. This stance raises issues of strategy and contingency, which are discussed in the particular setting of the mechanics industry in Kolhapur. Furthermore, exploring the relationship between determinism and contingency in life-paths raises important questions about how people construct their life stories in retrospect. Focusing on the case study of one family known over many years allows me to unravel the complex and subjective positionings at play in narrative research as it is mutually constituted by the story teller(s) and the anthropologist.

Introduction

It is a paradox that mobility studies purporting to analyse trends in socio-economic groups make use of quantitative data usually based on individual answers to questionnaires; as if 'collective' bodies were but the the total sum of individuals. The logic behind such methodology begs to be questioned. Rather than mere individual units, studying group social mobility should entail apprehending somewhat larger ones, such as the family. Size alone is not at issue here. What is, is that members of the same family are rarely chosen as respondents, random selection of sample preventing such an approach. Thus many quantitative studies tend to disregard the fact that mobility is not only a matter of individual agency but also of family praxis, and that individuals are embedded within family, occupational and local contexts. The first difficulty facing a study of socio-economic mobility is therefore one of articulating data pertaining to individuals with collective ones.

Another difficulty pertains to the methods and tools employed – particularly questionnaires. These often consider occupation as the 'sum of social status', thereby precluding interviewees from giving an account of the complexities of their situations (Bertaux and Thompson 1997). In addition, the socio-economic positioning of an informant at the time of data collection is often envisaged as a kind of final destination, leaving aside possible variations and even ups and downs in the course of a life-path.

Neither the assumptions underlying the collection of such data nor the data themselves indicate the contextual primacy and the contingency of people's lives; nor can they convey hesitations and twist-and-turns of life at different moments in time. Equally important and missing from this kind of 'objective' data is the 'qualitative stuff of social mobility', that is, the subjective representations that interviewees entertain of themselves in relation to shared notions of social achievement. Figures and graphs need to be reconciled with social agents' own understandings of what, if anything, constitutes social mobility and social achievement. This may also help us, social scientists, rethink the very categories of socio-economic mobility and social achievement. In this article, I explore the possibilities offered to this effect by the tool of *family* life history in the context of formerly Untouchable communities in western India, Maharashtra. While arguing in favour of family life histories as both resource and method in the Indian context, I reconsider the positivist functionalist stance dominant in studies of social mobility until the last decade. This stance raises issues of strategy and contingency, which are discussed in the particular setting of the mechanics industry in Kolhapur, southern Maharashtra. Furthermore, exploring the relationship between determinism and contingency in life-paths raises important questions about how people construct their life stories in retrospect[1]. Focusing on the case study of one family known over many years allows me to unravel the complex and subjective positionings at play in narrative research as it is mutually constituted by the story teller(s) and the researcher, here, the anthropologist.[2]

Social mobility, family histories, and strategies

Studies of social mobility have often been dominated by positivist functionalist theories of social stratification (Tumin 1985/1967, and before him, Sorokin), whereby large groups and sections of a given population move evenly upward owing to a variety of causal factors.[3] As Bertaux and Thompson rightly object, however, this pattern is rather rare. The vast majority of social agents 'circulate within' the social structure they see as given, and only a minority do create change, 'by either creating new spaces within the old structures, or moving' (1997, 2). The same has long obtained in Indian society. Despite the latter serving as a laboratory for studies of social stratification (Gupta 1991), comparatively few studies have focused on social mobility in terms other than statistical and economic.[4] In this paper, I draw upon the alternative methods developed by Bertaux, Wiame and Thompson over a decade ago for studying social and professional mobility (1997) in Europe. Breaking away from the argument and description dominated by 'the language of variables', their method shifted the analytical lens from the individual to the family. Here, I argue that allowing family life stories to (re-)enter sociological practice brings into relief the centrality of collective *and* individual representations and evaluations in shaping life-paths and, consequently, in any appraisal of socio-economic mobility.

Few studies of social mobility in India have so far focused on collective units such as families.[5] Yet, the 'family-based' generational perspective adopted by Bertaux and Bertaux-Wiame (1997) in their work on French society appears especially fruitful here, considering the lived reality of the Indian joint family principle even today. Particularly apposite is 'the idea of social status as an attribute of the family lead[ing] to the notion of family social trajectories as a sequence of social statuses for a "family"' (Bertaux and Bertaux-Wiame 1997, 64). Béteille similarly stresses the 'crucial if not decisive role' – far more active, says he, than caste – played by the

Indian family in the reproduction of social structure, including the structure of inequality (1991, 13). Of course, a familial focus is not meant to further any claim to primacy of the collective over the individual *in the Indian case*. The notion of a holistic society relegating any trace of individualism at its margins (Dumont 1970) has long been shattered, including with work on the emergence of individual consciousness in India (Kaviraj 2004). Rather than denying individuality to Indian people, my intention is to put this very individuation into perspective by replacing it within a wider familial framework. India is in this sense not exceptional; it shares commonalities with other societies, not least of all Britain. Thus, as regards education-facilitated upward mobility, the rise of an individual even in British society is equally influenced by a transgenerational family culture, in which the informant's grandfather, uncle, father, mother, grandmother, aunt, each played important parts (Thompson 1997, 56).[6] Furthermore, although the component parts of the family status, such as economic, cultural, interpersonal, geographic, etc., may be passed on, even economic capital, seemingly the most easily and directly transmitted, 'must undergo a metamorphosis if it is to be reappropriated by the following generation ... To become the subject of the heritage, the heir must act on it by leaving his or her mark on it' (Bertaux and Bertaux-Wiame 1997, 92). Consequently, even at the heart of family history, lies individual history.

Appraising family paths, then, brings into view varying scales and contexts often left out from sociological analysis (Lahire 1996). It also invites reconsideration of notions of strategy and contingency in relation to socio-economic mobility. It is usually assumed that particular communities as wholes embrace a certain type of education so as to access a certain type of job or to maintain the family business. Such general statements do not, however, account for any variation. In Kolhapur, the local ruler, Shahu Maharaj, is known to have promoted the rise of industrial activities among ex-Untouchables on a massive scale (Dahiwale 1989). Yet, zooming in at the level of each of the groups making up the category of 'ex-Untouchable', one finds different patterns from community to community. Amongst the three most important low castes to have set up industrial businesses, for instance, Mahars in the late 1990s were numerically dominant, whereas Mangs were less represented, though more than Chambhars. At the next level, one might therefore expect entire Mahar families to make strategic decisions with a view to entering or/and remaining in this line of business, especially given its ongoing worldwide expansion. With the same process repeating from one generation to the next, we would then collect nicely designed patterns of careful professional strategies, just as have been amply documented the world over, whether in South Asia or elsewhere. Less addressed in non-Euro-American contexts and more difficult to explain, however, is the variability of family paths and patterns encountered within the same community, *or even within the same family* (Benei 2005a).[7] These variations not only provide a different and nuanced picture from that of a uniformly specialized community. In addition, they question the overall supremacy generally accorded to rationality and strategy in people's lives.[8]

By exploring the complexities of family life-paths in the setting of technical and industrial education in Kolhapur at the end of the twentieth century, I aim to contribute to an understanding of socio-economic mobility that encompasses strategic and non-rational professional behaviours. Focusing on one extended family belonging to the entrepreneurial scene of Kolhapur mechanics industries, I hope to show how structural conditions as well as personal family histories together with individual idiosyncrases are closely interwoven in people's life-paths. The family members on whose life histories I concentrate might be taken as the archetype of blatant entrepreneurial success amongst scheduled castes, and indeed have been presented as such in a sociological study (Dahiwale 1989). But their case illuminates how within a given family, choices may be made according to individual potentialities, while other decisions are a matter of contingency. After all, '[c]hance ... must be part of even a fully determined world as soon as independent tracks of causation cross each other' (Bertaux and Thompson 1997, 17).

Of strategies and contingencies in the industrial setting of Kolhapur

Kolhapur, headquarters of the southernmost district of Maharashtra state (one of the most industrialized in India), is well known for its technical educational scene: even in the 1960s, before the all-Indian Kothari Commission report (1964–66) called for furthering higher technical training, the town housed one of the most important technical institutions in Maharashtra (Setu Madhava Rao 1960). In this respect, it overshadowed the rival city of Pune, often labelled the 'educational capital of Maharashtra'. Kolhapur's 'tradition' of technical schooling goes back to the early twentieth century when Chhatrapati Shahu Maharaj, then ruling the local kingdom, impulsed social reforms and developed education among the masses as part of a sweeping non-Brahmin movement of social protest in most of southern India. This movement had been initiated by Mahatma Jyotirao Phule in the late nineteenth century, and many of his followers in the first half of the twentieth century were inspired in founding 'educational societies' (*shikshan sanstha*), including technical institutions (O'Hanlon 1985; Benei 1997, 2005a).

Social mobility in the area was not dependent on the sole existence of educational society-founded schools. To be sure, some caste groupings took advantage of these, as they later did of positive discrimination policies and quotas. Yet, such an overall view fails to take stock of 'highly contrasting cultural micro-climates' (Bertaux and Bertaux-Wiame 1997, 65). Nor does it account for the apparent lack of strategizing among many families belonging in these same groups. How can one approach those life histories that do not appear to be the neat products of conscious acts and deliberate choices, and wherein family members, or entire families, do not plot their lives according to the strategic narrative theorised at a macro-level? Are these life narratives as meaningful for social scientists as those of others, apparently more self-willed?

At stake here is the combination of personal choice and contingency existing in a life-path. Take, for instance, 42-year-old Adhikrao. Asked how he had got his job at the reputed Ghatge Patil Industries (G.P.I.), the machinist grinder explained how he had been interviewed and selected by the company's officers while training at the Industrial and Training Institute (ITI) in Kolhapur. Why had he taken this private job in this particular company? The skilled technician enumerated a linear evential sequence from training to getting the job. 'Because of family responsibilities', after that, he had not tried for government service. In any case, there was a guarantee of a permanent job with G.P.I. One might ask: what was the extent of strategy in Adhikrao's choice? Can this even be called a choice? Or is it that our very questions induce a type of answer? By asking *why* someone *chose* a particular job, are we not distorting their account into an unduly willed narrative? How many are they, those who, like Adhikrao's colleague, 45-year-old Vasant, turner by profession, 'did not choose. This is not the question. There was this job here' ('*Mi nivadli nahi; ha prashna nahi; hi naukari hoti, ikade*')? How many are they, those who do not strategically move their pawns through their lives? How can the resource of family life history provide a useful means for dealing with these questions anthropologically and illuminate the tension between determinism and contingency?

Introducing the Pundat family: contingency or success strategy?

Life narratives are often governed by the same notion of a 'tale of unfolding moral purpose', a 'moral success story' (Wolf 1982, 5) undergirding the Western conception of History. The writing of individuals' biographies is similarly couched in the terms of acceptance of, or compliance with a notion of ordained succession of historic events, a *Geschichte*, or 'theory of narrative' (Bourdieu 1986, 69). Both types of history – the Great one and the auto-biographical – are governed by the same assumption of a (life) course guided by meaning and most of all, success. This begs the question of how meaningful the idea of success is in Indian society, especially to a former Untouchable.[9] Let me introduce you to the Pundat family (name changed). The Pundats were part of the small-scale industrial scene in Kolhapur. They owned two mechanics spare parts workshops where they prepared magnet covers for one of the biggest scooter companies in India. Today, this company has a distribution network covering 50 countries worldwide. Rough pieces were prepared in one workshop, while the finishing job was done in the other one. The business had been started some 30 years earlier by the father, Manohar, aged about 75 at the beginning of research. After being expanded, the family enterprise moved into the hands of two of the sons. The patriarch, however, still kept an eye on the business and his decision-power weighed much.

The Pundats lived jointly both professionally and privately. The family of 16 members owned a big house occupied by the patriarch and his wife, their three married sons and their wives and children, and occasionally their separated (married) daughter with her two children. All in-married women of the family were housewives and none had any economic input-bringing activities. My first encounter with the Pundats goes back to July 1996, when I first walked into one of their workshops, introduced by a sociology lecturer of Kolhapur University. After about an hour, I was left alone with the two brothers who offered to take me home to meet their father and the rest of the family.

The father, Manohar, diligently explained how as an 'automobile expert' he had taught his sons most of their trade. Manohar started as an assistant at S. Mandoli and Sons, an automobile company in Kolhapur, and worked there until 1947, ultimately starting his own workshop in 1952, specializing in Ford cars. At that time, he recalled, there were only four or five of them in Kolhapur. In 1974, he started an engineering workshop to manufacture automobile components, and later diversified production. How did Manohar, coming from a Bhangi (scavengers) caste, manage to become an 'automobile expert', especially in the 1950s, at a time when Nehru's India was only just beginning to implement its industrially orientated policy, and when entrepreneurship was limited to well-known business communities such as Jains, even in technical areas?[10] Here is where local conditions coupled with personal idiosyncrasy illuminate an informant's life and way of telling it. In the course of repeated long meetings over the following months, Manohar gladly proffered his own version of his success story. Through his narratives emerged a sense of self-achievement that was only tempered by his philosophical doubts and reflections as I got to know him and his family over many years, until 2003. What prompted Manohar to choose mechanics? For one, he liked studying, and particularly technical subjects. But, he also emphasized, similarly to many of his caste fellows and other ex-Untouchables, the absence of caste markers in the mechanics industry had been one of the main incentives for him: there was no question of caste there, nobody seemed to bother about it in the profession, perhaps because everybody belonged to lower sections of the population.[11]

Spatial mobility versus kin and caste ties

The workshop where Manohar trained as a young boy was situated opposite his home. This training pattern seems to have been fairly frequent in the town: people would entrust their sons to the skilled hands of a neighbour who owned a small factory or a workshop. Several decades later, Manohar's sons continued the pattern, employing as apprentices sons of neighbours who wanted their offspring to learn the trade. Recruitment for apprenticeship was thus rather informal and operated on spatial (neighbourhood) ties of trust, rather than social (kin or caste) ties. Space and spatial mobility are important here. They complement the necessary reconstruction of a life-path starting from a definition of social space as a set of positionings and movements within it (Bourdieu 1986, 71). Yet, space and spatial mobility are not only factors of socio-economic mobility, but also indicators of types of networks other than the usual kin and caste ones familiar in the Indian context. Indeed, space and movement were crucial determinants of success in Manohar's professional narratives, leading to the establishment of his family's socio-economic position in the mid-1990s. Originally from Kagal, a small town situated less than 20 km away, Manohar's parents held the traditional calling of their caste, that is, scavenging. As the birthplace of the heir to the Kolhapuri throne chosen for adoption in 1884, Kagal occupies a particular location in the symbolic geography of Kolhapur. Manohar's father was serving in the household of the young prince-to-be's paternal uncle (*kaka*). After his adoption, the young Shahu Maharaj settled in Kolhapur and in 1913–14 called his paternal uncle to come and live with him. The latter obliged, taking 'his own people' (those working for him) along. These settled in an area that has since borne the name of the benevolent ruler, hence 'Shahupuri'. According to the Pundat family, the buildings in that neighbourhood date back to this time. Manohar believed that by leaving Kagal his family was given an opportunity to uplift themselves (*'Amhi baher alo tyamule sudharlo'*). Contrary to the usual argument of social mobility along caste lines, he insisted that their uplift had been possible *through not living amidst fellow caste members and by mixing with people from the neighbourhood*, from other communities. These did not all consist of the lower sections of the population. In addition to Mahars, Mangs, and Dhors, members of intermediate status groups such as Dhangars, Marathas, Muslims, etc. lived in the area. What this example shows, then, is that if cohesive family culture typically becomes dynamic only in response to sharply changing social and economic contexts (Thompson 1997, 51; Leclerc-Olive 1997), it is important to acknowledge the fact that change also encompasses displacement and movement, in both social *and* spatial terms. What makes Manohar Pundat's account especially interesting is that it conceptualizes 'success' as the product of an evential sequence of social and spatial mobility.

All the adult family members carried with them an unmistakable air of self-respect and self-conscious social achievement, that was especially salient in our first conversation. Not only have Manohar and his three sons managed to get out of their caste calling but also to do well in setting up an independent business. This they certainly owe to their father's willpower and strength of character, combined with the opportunities offered by a locally changing socio-economic milieu in the first half of the century. Manohar would proudly state he had paid for his own studies with his own work at the mechanics workshop where he was trained. Yet, he also readily acknowledged an overall social welfare policy beneficial to Untouchables, not least in the field of education.

Educational achievements

Whereas his parents were illiterate, Manohar not only studied up to VIIth standard in Marathi medium at Kolhapur New Highschool: he went on another year in English medium (Vth standard), by which time he was 13 or 14 years old. As indicated above, Manohar paid for his own studies while working at the workshop opposite his house. His wife originated from Satara, another non-Brahmin stronghold. In my first meetings with the family, she appeared rather demure and shy, and her children asserted she had studied in Marathi up to VIIth standard. A year later, as we were chatting in the main room one evening, she bluntly told me she could neither read nor write; she signed with her thumb, she confessed amid some teasing and laughter on the part of her grandchildren. But Mahila Bai accepted this as the fate devolved her; these were different times, there was no money at home, even boys did not study because of the family's Untouchable status, so how else could have things been for her?

Things certainly changed at her children's generation, where caste and gender were no longer impediments. Manohar and Mahila had four children, three sons and one daughter. Both the eldest son and daughter were bright, according to their parents. Their socio-economic position had by then improved to the extent that they could afford to send both children to English-medium primary and secondary schools. Deepak, the eldest son aged 41 at the time of our first encounter in 1996, had even been sponsored by the Communist Party of India (CPI) to study further and graduate with a B.A. from Rajaram College, a rather elitist (though government) institution at the time. From there, he became a stenographer in geology at the Government Office. Sushila, the daughter, finished secondary school and got married. Her conjugal situation was such that she soon went back to live with her natal family, meanwhile working as a mid-rung clerk at the Municipality. The other two sons, Sudhir and Mohand, respectively aged 39 and 37, had been working for 20 years in the paternal factory. Their respective educational paths provide interesting contrasts further complicating decision-making processes with respect to gender: while both studied up to the secondary school certificate level, the eldest learnt in an English-medium school (the same as his elder brother) whereas the younger was sent to a Marathi (though private) institution after IIIrd standard as, he later explained, he 'had no interest' in school. No fees were paid for their education since the brothers by then benefited from the government reservations policy granted to Scheduled Castes.[12]

The same educational pattern repeats at the third generation. Sudhir, who studied in English medium, had one son and one daughter, respectively aged 11 and 7 at the beginning of research. The son went to the (very elite) New Modern English school. Fees, for which they received no aid, were Rs 70 per month. The daughter, allegedly because of her poor health, went to a Marathi-medium school, for which there were no fees. Mohand had two sons, aged 11 and 7. Although he himself had been educated in Marathi, both his children went to an English-medium school, the New Modern cited above. The fees therefore amounted to Rs 140 per month for both children.

Deepak, the eldest brother, had two sons, aged 13 and 11. The eldest one, 'because he does not like English' (and so the son repeated when asked in front of other family members), studied in Marathi medium, in the same school as his female cousin. His younger brother went to the New Modern English school. Altogether, the total amount spent monthly by the joint family on fees for English-medium schooling was Rs 280, a susbtantial sum at the time.

Education was not only central to overall betterment of the Pundat family's socio-economic status (thereby providing them access to idioms of citizenship heretofore unprecedented, see Benei 2005b), but the quality and medium of instruction were also deemed important. Consequently, the decision had been made to send all children and grandchildren to semi-private institutions rather than entrust them to government-only institutions, which were in disrepute. In this, Manohar, and later his sons, espoused the views of many parents of the middle and lower-middle classes. Opting for semi-private institutions therefore both reflected their status aspirations and facilitated their realization.[13] Similarly, the choice of medium of instruction was carefully calculated for the eight grandchildren, according to their declared potential. Regardless of gender, those deemed ablest were sent to English education, whereas the others studied in Marathi. English was important on all counts, not least for developing the family enterprise ('engineering books are written in English'), but also because of the general exposure it offered ('a lot more is written in English than in Marathi'). Thus, among Manohar's children and grandchildren, the reproduction of the family business had generated both inclusions and exclusions, determining the destiny of some children through a selective family process of advancing their career while strenghtening the indetermination of the destinies of others, congruently with a pattern familiar to sociologists of family histories in Europe (Bertaux and Bertaux-Wiame 1997, 83; Elliott 1997, 219; Andorka 1997).

Of fairy tales and anthropologists

Family life histories, then, appear a useful tool for qualitative approaches of social mobility. The difficulty, however, is that 'social mobility data are likely to incorporate their own degree of idealization' (Bertaux and Thompson 1997, 10). If life stories provide a finer texture of the complexities of interviewees' situations and life-paths than quantitative techniques, they nevertheless remain *discourses*, as previous anthropological research and more recent narrative research have insisted respectively (see Trahar 2008). The constitution of knowledge obtained through this type of enquiry has more to do with *Weltanschauungen*, with representations of the world (and of the self) than with a body of hard facts. Thus, while considering the diversity of possible life-paths crossing one another in a person's life, one must relinquish a mundane conception whereby informants' representations of their pasts to themselves would be real and tangible facts, of an objective world 'out there' (Pollner 1987). As is by now well known, informants' representations and discourses do *not* allow direct access to their minds; rather, they represent 'either an immediate or a mediate verbal text' (Crapanzano 1980). Consequently, the interaction between 'researcher' and 'informant' needs examining in the constitution of the latter's discourses about their life histories. These, at a second stage, will become 'doubly edited' (Crapanzano 1980, 1984) by the anthropologist, and reified into an 'enquiry-based object of knowledge'. To be sure, life histories should not be discarded as 'mere mundane speculations' (Pollner 1987). As Pollner himself insists, sociology can hardly do away with mundane reasoning. At the very least, though, one must account for the making of these life discourses.

What Janice Boddy notes about an 'appearance of resolution, a quasi-heroic outcome' (1997, 12) about the Somali woman whose life she was asked to co-edit holds true for a majority of the life histories that end up couched on paper. But, what lies behind the 'fairy tale' account is rarely glanced at. At first sight, if I stopped the narrative of the Pundat family in the late 1990s, the resulting picture would be one of unquestioned socio-economic achievement. The family have indeed gone a long way, from Manohar's illiterate parents earning their hand-to-mouth subsistence as scavengers in Kagal to his sons' and grandsons' English command and success in expanding the family business set up by him, not to mention those of his progeny entering government jobs, another source of status in India. Yet, a biography is often 'subterraneously worked' by something (dissimulation, illness, etc.) that may complexify – or even question – the happy narrative proffered (Leclerc-Olive 1997, 173). This something 'at work' may not always be subterraneous, but, rather, 'overground' and conscious; awareness of it may even have been enhanced in the course of repeated telling of the story, either to oneself, to family members, or to the anthropologist. This calls for further exploration.

Naming and the erasure of untouchability

While education and occupation are often deemed markers of 'significant social achievement' (Elliott 1997, 201), other markers pertain more specifically to background and belonging. In the Indian context, they, of course, include caste. Manohar Pundat prided himself upon having overcome his birth status of untouchability. The erasure of untouchability, for himself and his family, underlay his biographical narratives over the years that I got to know him. Manohar had a very acute sense of his socio-economic achievement rising from an Untouchable caste to that of an 'ordinary' man with fully fledged autonomy and dignity attached to his newly attained socio-economic status. This was best epitomized by his regular reference to the question his granddaughter had once asked him. At the end of our very first – two-hour-long – interview, Manohar had concluded that governing his life had been extracting himself out of his caste condition by setting up his own independent means of livelihood. Although untouchability was officially abolished in Kolhapur in 1919, Manohar spoke of the hard time Untouchables had undergone throughout the twentieth century, whether in professional or other areas of social life. Using the Marathi word (*asprushyata*), he recalled in a matter-of-fact yet emphatic tone how 'untouchability' governed every aspect of Untouchables' lives to the extent that they had no right to a barber's services; of all the other castes only a doctor could touch them. Whether Manohar's account is factually 'true' or not is undoubtedly important for the comparative insight it offers into twentieth-century Kolhapur, especially given the widespread idea of substantial help to, and promotion of 'the downtrodden' under the benevolent rule of Shahu Maharaj. Yet more interesting is how Manohar represented this Untouchable past to himself, so as to distantiate himself better from it. Today, he proudly added, his granddaughter asks him what 'untouchability' means. That his granddaughter, aged seven at the beginning of research, should not understand the very word that had designated the stigma attached to the people of his condition for so many centuries (Manohar did have a notion of long duration) was to him evidence of its successful erasure, at least in his own family. School, he reckoned, was now the only place where the notion was ever used, not as defining daily experience, but as a 'word' that pupils learnt as part of a history curriculum, in which featured the good deeds of Kolhapur's royal benefactor, Shahu Maharaj (Benei 1999, 2008).

As I became more intimate with the family, however, I grew increasingly aware of the ambiguities – fragility, even – of the family's sense of social achievement. Manohar and his family variously displayed the attributes of self-conscious socio-economic achievement in many areas of their lives, not least of all through their patterns of consumption. From material goods ranging to a solid concrete modern house with all the commodities one could wish for in India at the time to the possession of scooters, telephones, and so on, to comfortable dietary and sartorial habits, their modes of consumption both indicated and facilitated their socio-economic upward mobility. The one thing none of this had changed, however, ... was their surname. In the urban setting of Kolhapur and in the composite neighbourhood in which they lived, this indication of their former caste status may not have mattered so much; at least judging from Manohar's early accounts. Yet, these may have operated as voiceovers over possible echoes of other, more sensitively disruptive narratives. If Manohar's dominant stance was deliberately positive, along the lines of a successful erasure of his and his kin's untouchability, it gradually appeared to stand in contrast to that of his sons' and daughters-in-law. They were the ones now navigating their way into the rest of Kolhapuri society. Their modes of consumption made them pass as ordinary middle-class citizens; but their surname still betrayed their humble origins. That this was most crucially revealed through the painful confrontation suffered by the women of the house made it even more of an issue, given Indian women's role as epitomes of the family.

A few years into research, I once accompanied the ladies of the house (the three sisters-in-law) on one of few occasions for them to go out, that is, a much-awaited shopping trip. The trip's value was clearly not only economic or socially symbolic, but also that of a personal treat. The ladies had donned some of their best saris, matched with impractically heeled chappals and bangles and other fancy jewelry, adding a touch of talcum powder to their respectable faces. Taking rickshaws to be driven around the 'posh' part of town, stopping for ice-cream and sweets in a parlour on the way, leisurely walking the street and into the shops, were pleasures integral to the outing and meant to be enjoyed to the full in the absence of any male supervision. So was the social interaction in each store. Through the many snippets of conversation, each site provided a space for the ladies to display, enact and perform their social status and respectability ... until, in a lingerie boutique (one of the very few then in Kolhapur), the storekeeper, another respectable lady, asked for the family.'s surname. Sudden blank in the conversation. Some hesitation. Sharmila, the most vivacious of the sisters-in-law, responded with aplomb, 'Pundat'. 'Pundat?' repeated the salesperson with unmistakable puzzlement. 'Pundat?' Her tone of voice by now carried an incredulous nuance of social suspicion. 'Yes, Pundat'. 'Oh, and where are you from? You aren't from Kolhapur, then, are you? Or are you?' No such name as Pundat was known locally, and what made it sound so odd was its auditory proximity to the Brahmin 'Pandit'. The sisters-in-law muttered some explanation as to the origins going back to a nearby village, and made their exit rather faster than socially appropriate. In the rickshaw on the way back, the mood had become sullen, as if this exchange had ruined the whole enjoyment of the outing. What was it to this woman, anyway? Why ask such questions? Not a shop to return to. It was then, that squeaks in the well-oiled narrative of social success began acquiring volume. For the issue of the name had apparently been one for some time already. In the days and weeks that followed, it was to gain prominence, especially through male voicing. There followed many a discussion between father and sons as to the feasibility and desirability of officially changing the family's surname. Ironically, contrary to well-documented trends, the intended move was not governed by a desire to benefit from the affirmative action policy implemented in favour of former Untouchables since Independence ('reservations policy'), quite the opposite: it was meant to once and for all shed any possibility of being defined by untouchability and/or economic 'backwardness'.

The dialogic construction of 'untouchability'

I have already hinted at the implications of repeated telling of one's life story, either to oneself, family members, or to the anthropologist. I now want to dwell on these implications. Although it is difficult to assess the extent to which the recourse to the same informants by various researchers affect the latter's worldview, it can reasonably be expected to impact on their own representations of themselves and their life histories. The Pundat family was introduced to me by a sociology lecturer who had worked with them for a few years on entrepreneurship among Scheduled Castes/Classes. The reiterated interviews among family members may have contributed to reinforcing self-representations as 'ex-Untouchables', if only so as to distantiate themselves further from their original condition and/or underprivileged status. Elliott's transposition of Bourdieu's analyses of Kabyle society to Scots and Scottish migrants might well apply to formerly Untouchable groups: 'For subordinated peoples there is an urgent need for recognition, for symbolic capital through which can be made assertions of worth against insistent denial and the pervasive representation of inferiority' (1997, 226).

Thus, through his long and repeated interaction with the university professor, himself of ex-Untouchable background, Mr. Pundat had had a heightened possibility of looking at his life and reconstructing it to suit his present situation, working it into a coherent whole through the motifs of success and self-achievement that ultimately appeared dominant in his life. When I first met him, the patriarch was quite ready and willing to let me partake of his interpretative recollections; as if, I somehow felt, a meeting with a foreign social scientist further confirmed his important social trajectory. Such a meeting operated as added value to the worthy long way he had gone from his Bhangi destitute childhood to his enterprising ownership at the time of his retirement, when he was able to transmit more than a trade to two of his sons, but also capital, in economic, cultural and social terms (Bourdieu). Also striking at first was the 'matter-of-factness' in the relating of his entire life story, no doubt for an umpteenth time. It was as if a string of events over a lifetime had been constructed over and over again and made meaningful through multiple interviews, enabling their teller to accrue the distance between himself and his past through conceptualizing it, thus (re)constructing a solidly consistent view of its determinants.[14] This is of course not to say that Mr. Pundat had 'served' me but a heated up version of a dish cooked long ago with the help of a local sociologist. To be sure, objectification and self-reflection do exist within every culture (Rabinow 1977) and all social actors in some way or other represent their own lives to themselves (Wright Mills 1940). Yet, this kind of self-conscious recounting is arguably less common and its present consistency owes much to the repeated encounters with the erstwhile-mentioned sociologist. For this reason, it is only fair to acknowledge the dia- (or tri-, in the present case) logic quality of this (re)construction; not only to avoid the easy narrative of fairy tale in studies of social mobility, but also to fairly tell the complexity, richness, and ambiguities of all life histories as retrospective accounts. For, in the end, this very richness and complexity is what makes them such productive resources for any comparative endeavour.

Notes

1. See Vincent's insightful study (1997) of unfulfilled expectations and lost potentials among Britishers in the first half of the twentieth century.
2. For an overview of the recent trend of 'narrative research' and how it can contribute to studies of social mobility as well as comparative and international educational research, see Sheila Trahar (2008). Thanks are due to the two reviewers for their perceptive comments and helpful suggestions.
3. More rarely are studies concerned with downward mobility (Benei and Kennedy 1997).
4. For notable exceptions, see the work of Johnny Parry on the Bhilai steel plant and Jan Breman on labour migration as well as the pioneering work of André Béteille (1971).
5. See Donner (2006, 2008) and Fuller and Narasimhan (2007, 2008) for recent exceptions.
6. See Evans's (2006) study of lower middle-class children for a contemporary example, and Willis's (1981/1977) for an earlier demonstration, both in the English context.
7. Lahire (1997) discusses similar micro-climates in educational settings and achievements among French schoolchildren.
8. Landy (1995) incorporates 'non-rational' elements into his account of 'farmers' logics'.
9. Lack of space prevents me from dwelling on the Marathi semantic field of 'yash', the term translating as 'success'.
10. Many of the technical colleges founded prior to the 1960s in southern Maharashtra were initiated by Jain industrialists and engineers.
11. Even years later, out of the 22 workers employed in the two workshops, 30% belonged to Other Backward Castes, 25% to Scheduled Castes, 25% were Muslims and the remaining 20% lower-class Marathas.
12. The women married into the family had all studied in Marathi medium, but laid great emphasis on the usefulness of English in their children's future careers.
13. See Donner (2006) for a similar observation with reference to Bengali middle-class families' choice of English-medium education in Calcutta.
14. As Leclerc-Olive writes (1997, 75): 'C'est leur discordance [des événements] jamais totalement réduite qui pousse la personne à en faire (à nouveau?) un récit et qu'elle espère tirer de ces rencontres une plus grande maîtrise symbolique de ce que fut sa vie, ne serait-ce que par le biais d'une mise en ordre chronologique des événements qui la structurent'.

References

Andorka, R. 1997. Social mobility in Hungary since the Second World War: Interpretations through surveys and through families histories. In *Pathways to social class: A qualitative approach to social mobility,* ed. D. Bertaux and P. Thompson, 259–98. Oxford: Clarendon Press.

Benei, V. 1997. Education, industrialization and socio-economic development: Some reflections for further sociological research in Western India. In *Industrial decentralization and urban development: A workshop on a Most/Unesco research project,* ed. Véronique Benei and Loraine Kennedy, 101–8. Pondy Papers in Social Sciences, no. 23. Pondichéry, Karthala: Institut français de Pondichéry.

Benei, V. 1999. Reappropriating colonial documents in Kolhapur (Maharashtra): Variations on a nationalist theme. *Modern Asian Studies* 33: 913–50.

Benei, V. 2005a. Of languages, passions and interests: Education, regionalism and globalization in Maharashtra, 1800–2000. In *Globalizing India: Locality, nation and the world,* ed. Jackie Assayag and Chris Fuller, 141–62. London: Anthem Press.

Benei, V., ed. 2005b. *Manufacturing citizenship: Education and nationalism in Europe, South Asia, and China.* London and New York: Routledge.

Benei, V. 2008. *Schooling passions: Nation, history, and language in contemporary western India.* Stanford, CA: Stanford University Press.

Bertaux, D., and I. Bertaux-Wiame. 1997. Heritage and its lineage: A case history of transmission and social mobility over five generations. In *Pathways to social class: A qualitative approach to social mobility,* ed. D. Bertaux and P. Thompson, 62–97. Oxford: Clarendon Press.

Bertaux, D., and P. Thompson, eds. 1997. Introduction. In *Pathways to social class: A qualitative approach to social mobility,* ed. D. Bertaux and P. Thompson, 1–31. Oxford: Clarendon Press.

Béteille, A. 1971. *Caste, class and power: Changing patterns of stratification in a Tanjore village.* Berkeley and London: University of California Press.

Béteille, A. 1991. The reproduction of inequality: Occupation, caste and family. *Contributions to Indian Sociology* 25, no. 1: 3–28.

Boddy, J. 1997. Writing *Aman. Anthropology Today* 13, no. 3: 9–14.

Bourdieu, P. 1986. L'illusion biographique. *Actes de la Recherche en Sciences Sociales* 62–63: 69–72.

Crapanzano, V. 1980. *Tuhami: Portrait of a Moroccan.* Chicago and London: Chicago University Press.

Crapanzano, V. 1984. Life-histories. *American Anthropologist* 86: 953–60.

Dahiwale, S.M. 1989. *Emerging entrepreneurship among Scheduled Castes of contemporary India: A study of Kolhapur City.* New Delhi: Concept Publishing Company.

Donner, H. 2006. Committed mothers and well-adjusted children: Privatisation, early-years education and motherhood in Calcutta. *Modern Asian Studies* 40: 371–95.

Donner, H. 2008. *Domestic goddesses: Maternity, globalisation and middle-class identity in contemporary India.* Aldershot, UK: Ashgate.

Dumont, L. 1970. The individual as an impediment to sociological comparison and Indian history. In *Religion/politics and history in India,* 133–50. Paris: Mouton.

Elliott, B. 1997. Migration, mobility, and social process: Scottish migrants in Canada. *Pathways to social class: A qualitative approach to social mobility,* ed. D. Bertaux and P. Thompson, 198–229. Oxford: Clarendon Press.

Evans, G. 2006. *Educational failure and working class white children in Britain.* London: Palgrave.

Fuller, C.J., and H. Narasimhan. 2007. Information technology professionals and the new-rich middle class in Chennai (Madras). *Modern Asian Studies* 41: 121–50.

Fuller, C.J., and H. Narasimhan. 2008. From landlords to software engineers: Migration and urbanization among Tamil Brahmans. *Comparative Studies in Society and History* 50, no. 1: 170–96.

Gupta, D., ed. 1991. *Social stratification.* Delhi: Oxford University Press.

Kaviraj, S. 2004. The invention of private life: A reading of Sibnath Sastri's *Autobiography*. In *Telling lives in India: Biography, autobiography, and life history,* ed. David Arnold and Stuart Blackburn, 83–115. Bloomington: Indiana University Press.

Lahire, B. 1996. La variation des contextes en sciences sociales – remarques épisté-mologiques. *Annales HSS* 2: 381–407.

Lahire, B. 1997. *Tableaux de famille.* Paris: Seuil.

Landy, F. 1995. *Paysans du sud de l'Inde.* Paris and Pondichéry, Karthala: Institut français de Pondichéry.

Leclerc-Olive, M. 1997. *Le dire de l'événement (biographique).* Paris: Presses Universitaires du Septentrion.

O'Hanlon, R. 1985. *Caste, conflict and ideology: Mahatma Jotirao Phule and low caste protest in nineteenth-century Western India.* Cambridge, UK: Cambridge University Press.

Pollner, M. 1987. *Mundane reason: Reality in everyday and sociological discourse.* Cambridge: Cambridge University Press.

Rabinow, P. 1977. *Reflections on fieldwork in Morocco.* London: University of California Press.

Setu Madhava Rao (ed.). 1960. *Gazetteer of India, Maharashtra State, Kolhapur Districts* (revised edition). Bombay: Directorate of Government Printing, Stationery and Publications.

Thompson, P. 1997. Women, men, and transgenerational family influences in social mobility. In *Pathways to social class: A qualitative approach to social mobility,* ed. D. Bertaux and P. Thompson, 32–61. Oxford: Clarendon Press.

Trahar, S. 2008. 'It starts with once upon a time…' *Compare* 38: 259–66.

Tumin, M.M. 1985/1967. *Social stratification: The forms and functions of inequality.* London: Prentice-Hall.

Vincent, D. 1997. Shadow and reality in occupational history: Britain in the first half of the twentieth century. In *Pathways to social class: A qualitative approach to social mobility*, ed. D. Bertaux and P. Thompson, 98–123. Oxford: Clarendon Press.

Willis, P. 1977/1981. *Learning to labour: How working class kids get working class jobs*. Farnborough, UK and New York: Saxon House and Columbia University Press.

Wolf, E. 1982. *Europe and the people without history*. London: University of California Press.

Wright Mills, C. 1940. Situated actions and vocabularies of motive. *American Sociological Review* 5: 904–13.

Marginal returns: re-thinking mobility and educational benefit in contexts of chronic poverty

Bryan Maddox

School of International Development, University of East Anglia, Norwich, UK

> As a result of chronic poverty many people in South Asia experience poor quality schooling, interrupted schooling, or no schooling at all. People affected by poverty face multiple constraints on wellbeing, which typically include informal employment, low wages and poor health. In such contexts the benefits and, more specifically, the 'returns' to education are not easily observed. Standard measures of educational attainment (such as primary school completion, years of schooling, literacy rates) are ill-suited to capture and understand such benefits. Similarly, data on income from formal employment is likely to be unsuitable. The paper argues that concepts of educational benefit and mobility have to be re-thought in contexts of chronic poverty to capture the 'marginal returns' in situations of constraint and vulnerability. The paper illustrates this argument with ethnographic vignettes of uses of literacy by non-schooled adults in Bangladesh.

Introduction

Educational and occupational life-histories often involve mobility – processes of dislocation and adjustment, the learning and embodiment of new identities, knowledge and languages. The dynamics of schooling and mobility are often inter-related, as cosmopolitan urban centres act as nodal points of educational aspiration. Corbett (2007) has argued that there is a 'migration imperative' in rural education, drawing people away from home communities, cultures, livelihoods and familiar environments. This logic of mobility is intricately tied with projects of modernity and development, and how we evaluate the success of educational interventions. The economic literature on the returns to education tends to evaluate the benefits in terms of occupational mobility and increased income. Non-monetary benefits are considered hard to quantify and compare. Sociological commentaries on educational benefits (or lack of) are similarly concerned with progressive change as mobility, whether in terms of status, income or occupational identity (Jeffrey, Jeffery, and Jeffery 2008). Much of this writing prioritises formality; the formality of educational credentials (whether qualifications of years of schooling), and the formal aspects of labour market participation as salaried employment.

The paper examines an alternative perspective, arguing that in contexts of chronic poverty we need understandings of educational benefit and mobility to capture the marginal returns that are available to those with minimum levels of educational achievement. These are people who live in conditions of poverty, have no formal educational credentials, and few opportunities for formal employment. Nevertheless, the paper presents ethnographic vignettes of how rudimentary adult literacy learning in Bangladesh impacts on people's lives. As the paper argues, they benefit from tangible returns that are observable through ethnographic analysis. The paper concludes by suggesting some implications of this for the ways in which we conceptualise and measure educational returns and mobility.

To theorise educational mobility in conditions of chronic poverty we must recognise the ways in which socio-economic constraints and vulnerability reduce people's life chances. This requires sensitivity to the conditions that reproduce poverty and the potential for educationally derived improvements to wellbeing in contexts where there is little prospect of formal paid employment. Chronic poverty is understood, following the Chronic Poverty Research Centre (2008), as multiple and persistent conditions of human insecurity, typically including income poverty, under-nutrition, poor health, and various aspects of entitlement failure (e.g. limited citizenship, poor or non-existent services). The Chronic Poverty Research Centre (2008, 9) estimates that 320–443 million people are chronically poor, with the most widespread poverty being in South Asia (126–176 million), and sub-Saharan Africa (124–159 million). The phenomenon has been intensively researched in recent years to produce clearer understanding of its characteristics and dynamics (e.g. see Hulme and Shepherd 2003; Hulme and Green 2005; Baulch and Davis 2008).

Human insecurity on this scale results from contextual influences (e.g. economic global conditions, environmental change, labour-relations) that are beyond the control of individual actors and households. Conditions of low pay, employment insecurity and seasonality are typical characteristics of labour market informality that is widespread in South Asia and sub-Saharan Africa (Paci and Serneels 2007). They present significant obstacles to mobility. Chronic poverty traps people in conditions where opportunities for escape are limited, and where multiple risks of downward descent into destitution are a feature of every-day life (Sen and Hulme 2007; Khan and Seeley 2005; Chronic Poverty Research Centre 2008). Faced with such vulnerability, people may 'trade off' short-term security for long-term mobility. Wood (2003) argues that chronically poor people may 'choose' to make a 'Faustian Bargain', to live with conditions of exploitation and inequality, rather than risking all to change their social order. The opportunity for 'escape' through migration also entail risks for the poor. It may be viewed as a last chance strategy (e.g. at times of flood or drought, or seasonal of employment), and may lead to the dissolution of the family as a viable social or economic unit (Seeley, Maddox, and Islam 2006).

Marginal returns

> Anything worth measuring, in human quality of life, is difficult to measure. (Nussbaum 2000, 240)

How then do we evaluate educational interventions where little or no upward mobility has been achieved? The implications of chronic poverty for educational achievement have received insufficient attention (Rose and Dyer 2006). Conditions of chronic poverty are challenging for educationalists who are committed to the idea that schooling should improve people's wellbeing, and create opportunities for occupational mobility. This challenge means re-thinking the construction of educational benefits *as* upward mobility. Assumptions of inter-generational mobility through education require similar caution. The inter-generational transfer of poverty remains salient in countries such as Bangladesh, which have experienced significant improvements in educational access and quality, but where poverty remains a cause and outcome of low educational achievement (Rahman 2006; Quisumbing 2007; Baulch and Davis 2008).

The challenge is to develop contextually sensitive understandings and analysis of educational benefits and mobility that capture the ways that education and learning contribute to poor people's lives. This requires revision of existing approaches to educational returns. Psacharopoulos and Patrinos describe consistent, 'tangible and measurable returns to investment in education' (2004, 118) that are internationally observed. However, it is not clear that all returns to education are equally tangible and measurable (Robinson-Pant 2008). The rates of return literature supports the case for educational investment. However, an emphasis on the consistency of returns conceal evidence of variation that may have equally important policy implications. Pritchett (2001) and Dufflo (2001) investigate the dynamics of educational returns, and describe significant variation between locations and over time. In respect of 'marginal' rates of return (the return from small, additional amounts of education), there is also evidence of variation in returns across different levels of education. Trostel argues that while most economic literature 'implicitly assumes that the marginal rate of return is constant over all levels of education', there is evidence of 'significant nonlinearity in the rate of return to schooling' (2005, 191). Noting variation in returns to education, Trostel describes studies that indicate higher returns at low levels of education, evidence of diminishing marginal returns in some cases (2005, 192), and s-shaped variation, where marginal returns are greatest in the middle range of educational achievement (2005, 199). The implications and dynamics of such variation have not yet been fully explored for developing countries, or in terms of the implications for how we understand educational returns for chronically poor people. It is clear that contextual variation in factors such as labour market conditions will impact on returns. However, there are major methodological and conceptual challenges in extending this analysis to chronically poor people – not least because of the difficulty in obtaining reliable data.

Glewwe (2002) describes a series of methodological difficulties in the production of data on educational returns. These include school factors (e.g. variations in teacher and school quality, grade repetition, drop out), and the implications of learner characteristics including cognitive ability. Glewwe draws attention to the limitations involved in any analysis that relies too heavily on formal educational achievements, and on income from formal employment. He argues that measures of income used in the analysis of returns should include income derived from self-employment and family workers (while acknowledging that such data are difficult to obtain) and notes that in Bangladesh 62% of employment is self-employment (2002, 467). This may be a conservative estimate as other studies argue that informal employment in South Asia is around 90% (Bremen 1996; Harriss-White 2003). There is therefore a risk that studies of returns to education compare the most 'reliable' data that is easiest to obtain, and as such tell us little (or even misrepresent) the potential benefits of education, and the scope for socio-economic mobility for chronically poor people.

A parallel argument can be made about the difficulties involved in capturing educational achievement for people who have dropped out of school, attended irregularly, or those who benefit from informal learning. The evidence suggests that in some contexts there may be high rates of return to education for people with low levels of educational attainment. These groups form a significant proportion of the population in low-income countries. They are the groups targeted by educational policies, but we have insufficient evidence of their educational returns. There some valid reasons for this. It is hard to obtain reliable (and comparable) data on educational attainment for the groups with the lowest achievements in education. In situations where no formal credentials are obtained, years of school enrolment may be an unreliable measure of educational attainment because of variations in learning achievement and school quality.[1]

With reference to the economic concept of marginal returns, the argument below provides an ethnographic example of learning at the most basic end of the educational spectrum, in informal adult literacy classes that are not captured by measures of credentials or years of schooling. The longitudinal research that informs the paper was able to examine such learning through a sustained process of participant observation, interviews and informal literacy assessment. The marginality considered relates to the types of economic returns experienced by chronically poor people, and describes the small-scale, almost intangible benefits obtained in self-employment for people who are living at or below the poverty line.

The vignettes below are intended to extend this discussion, and contribute to an inter-disciplinary dialogue. They explore the idea that for people living in chronic poverty, the analysis of educational benefit and mobility must be sufficiently sensitive to lived experience, to observe the ways in which apparently small-scale benefits may have important implications for wellbeing. Such returns may be evaluated in relation to people's ability to sustain wellbeing, their resilience to cope with insecurity, rather than solely in terms of their ability to 'escape' from poverty. Experienced in these ways, educational returns operate as an insurance against a fall into deeper poverty or destitution (Dercon 2004). Such small-scale benefits may well operate well below the conceptual radar of the present economic literature on 'rates of return'.

The vignettes build on my earlier work where I demonstrate how small-scale benefits of literacy can be captured in ethnographic research (Maddox 2007, 2008). The vignettes use pseudonyms, but in other respects, have attempted to portray the characters and facts as accurately as possible. The people discussed are intended to provide illustrative case studies of learning and mobility. They are not intended as a commentary on the efficacy of adult literacy campaigns in Bangladesh, which are subject to some debate (e.g. Ahmed, Nath, and Ahmed 2003). The examples build on a literature that uses ethnographic methods to capture small-scale, local insights into chronic poverty that may be missed by large-scale analysis (Hulme 2004). They illustrate how micro-ethnographic analysis (based on in-depth interviews, life-histories, and narrative form) can inform our understanding of learning and mobility, and demonstrate the scope for ethnographic research to support quantitative analysis on the dynamics of chronic poverty (Hulme and Green 2005). Informed by a 'social practice' model of literacy, the vignettes focus on instrumental benefits and specifically on the links between literacy practices and economic wellbeing. They build on the critical ethnographic tradition of the New Literacy Studies (Street 1995), while recognising the scope for intrinsic and instrumental benefits of literacy as an aspect of human development (Maddox 2008). The paper contributes to the wider international ethnographic literature, which include other descriptions of people who benefit from fragile levels of literacy (e.g. Kell 1999; Zavala 2008; Blommaert 2008).

The research context

The fieldwork that informs this paper took me from urbanised centres of Western Europe to the rural north-west of Bangladesh. I conducted 12 months of ethnographic fieldwork (1997–1999) followed by a return visit to the same location in 2005. The research took place in and around a small market town, and focused on how non-schooled adults learn and use literacy and numeracy in their every-day life. I worked with small rural communities, but the patterns of every-day life involved daily travel to the local town. On my arrival in the area, it was the movement of people that impressed me. They crammed into buses, on bicycles and rickshaws. Many (including children), because of poverty, started their day with a long cycle or walk on dusty paths. The town was a hub of economic and cultural activity, with a large bazaar and weekly livestock market. It was home to mosques, courts, shops, restaurants, and cinemas, government and non-governmental offices, land sub-registry, training centres, and educational institutions; a large high school, several *madrasas*, and a girls' college.

North-west Bangladesh is one the poorest regions of the country. It is affected by high seasonal unemployment, food deficits, poor public health and income poverty (Baulch and Davis 2008). Living there, in conditions of chronic poverty, is a harsh and vulnerable existence (Save the Children 2005). The area suffers from cycles of flooding and drought which accentuate seasonal unemployment and out-migration. Low wages for agricultural labour and 'off-farm' rural occupations (e.g. from rickshaw pulling, sewing) trap people in conditions of chronic poverty.

The area, like the rest of Bangladesh, has a strong literate culture, and literacy plays a key role in many social practices. Social participation, interactions with dominant government and non-government institutions, access to entitlements and resources are textually mediated. There is a strong vernacular literacy culture, with widespread uses in religious activity, daily economic activities, credit and communication. But while literacy has significant social utility, it is not a panacea against social disadvantage (Street 1995). With these considerations in mind, the vignettes below describe how literacy practices and capabilities of non-schooled people contribute to wellbeing.

Kamrul

> Kamrul works as a rickshaw puller. In his mid-twenties he lives with his wife, three young children, and his mother. His father died several years ago, and now he is the main income earner. By Bangladeshi standards the family are not extremely poor. They own a small home with a vegetable garden and grow a little rice in a nearby field. They have space for a few ducks, and share in a cow that they are rearing. Nevertheless, in terms of cash, they are highly dependent on Kamrul's income. Kamrul owns his rickshaw and works long hours, but his earnings are rarely more than enough to cover the family's financial needs. Having become literate through a combination of self-study and adult literacy class, Kamrul keeps detailed records of income and expenditure, and credit arrangements in a pocket notebook. As he shows me there are many days when his income is insufficient to cover the cost of the family's food. Rickshaw pulling is particularly hard in the more rural areas away from the centre of town, with their sandy unpaved roads. The family's wellbeing is entirely dependent on his ability to stay sufficiently healthy for this work. That is not easy, like other rickshaw pullers, he has to eat low-cost foods (such as stale bread from one of the town's bakeries), as other foods are too expensive. Working as a rickshaw puller Kamrul earned 80–100 taka on a good day (in 2005). Items such as repairs on his rickshaw and medical costs of his family, were

enough to use up any surplus. Working from the town bazaar, his income was greater on market days, but in the agricultural off-season and during times of flood, he travels to the city of Noakhali, where he works in rickshaw pulling and as a day-labourer. There he can earn 150 taka per day – enough to cover his costs and save a little to take home. Kamrul describes how his literacy has helped in such journeys. When travelling, he is confident about reading bus tickets (which include seat numbers), and is able to read road signs and notices along the way. Other, less financially secure, migrants have to travel on top of buses, or in the case of extremely poor migrants, a perilous journey, clinging to the rear end of the bus. These subtle differences mark out the terrain of social mobility and decline for the rural poor. While he works in Noakhali, Kamrul lives in a 'hostel' where he shares living costs with the other residents. There are many costs for migrant rickshaw pullers to cover, including food and water, rents, and the informal 'taxes'. Kamrul records his income and expenditure, and manages the financial records in the hostel as few others there are literate. He is able to communicate through letters home (or if necessary, through the phone shops that are now an integral part of life in Bangladesh). His wife is not literate, but asks a neighbour to read for her. Kamrul also keeps in touch with events in his home area through reading newspapers.

For Kamrul, learning literacy has been useful for life management, and coping with poverty. His records of income and expenditure, and debts, have enabled him to manage and evaluate his economic activities more carefully. It has also helped with his physical mobility, increasing his confidence and abilities involved in seasonal migrations. I have known Kamrul since 1997. He is a warm and friendly character, who loves his family dearly. He and his wife have three young girls. As the family has grown their living costs have increased, but their income has not. The costs associated with family illness have increased their debt burden. One of his girls attends school, and the others will follow. Kamrul is sufficiently literate to help them with school work (reading Bangla and English), and wants all his girls to do well, but only time will tell whether the family income is sufficient to cover the costs of schooling and break that dimension of intergenerational poverty. Kamrul knows that working as a rickshaw puller has taken its toll on his body (the main source of income). He understands the associated vulnerability, but lacks sufficient occupational mobility to do anything about it.

Halima

Halima had never attended school. When the women's literacy class opened in the community she attended erratically due to the demands of work, and because of her husband's unhappiness about her attendance. An agricultural labourer, Halima worked as a share-cropper, growing vegetables, wheat and tobacco in fields surrounding her home. Her husband was not literate ('not even able to sign his name') and works as a rickshaw van puller (a rickshaw, but with a flat back, for transporting people and goods). When I first got to know her she lived with her two children (one boy and one girl). Her husband often suffered from ill-health and spent many days at home in bed. By 2005 her son had left home to work in a restaurant in town, and the girl married early and left home. They regretted sending their children away, but did not have enough income to feed them. Halima showed me photographs of her children that were pinned to their wall inside her thatched home. Despite resistance from her husband, Halima learned elementary literacy in the adult literacy class. She talked openly about the value of learning, and the confidence that it had given her to 'hold' and read written texts. She joked (making sure that her husband could hear), that now that she was literate, the next thing she would learn would be how to ride a bicycle. One of the first texts that Halima showed me was a record of income and expenditure associated with her wheat harvest. When I met her in 2005 her situation had declined considerably. She had lost her share-cropping land.

Her husband was ill with a rasping cough. Socially isolated, and in economic crisis, they were close to destitution. They sold the small piece of land on which their small home was built, and while I was there, used the cash to invest in a small roadside shop. Halima was to be the shop keeper. She felt that the literacy and numeracy she had gained were sufficient to enable her to manage the shop.

Since I got to know Halima in 1997, her life-course is similar to many people struggling with chronic poverty. Her life is desperately hard and her income is dependent not only on her and her husband's ability to labour, and cycles of seasonality, but on the kinds of social relationships they can establish in their community. Halima, now in her late thirties looks much older. The loss of their homestead, their share-cropping land, and the fragmentation of their family reflect wider patterns of downward mobility among the rural poor (Seeley, Maddox, and Islam 2006). Like so many other rural women, her physical mobility is extremely limited, but is not insignificant. When she was able to access share-cropping land Halima's income depended on her ability to move within the local community, to the homes of friends, and to nearby fields. This involved a careful negotiation of the terms of purdah. This limited physical mobility was essential to her livelihood and wellbeing. Attending the literacy class (five minutes walk from her home) involved degrees of physical and social freedom that were perceived as a challenge to patriarchal gender-relations. Ironically, her literacy not only enabled her to keep better records of agricultural income and expenditure (which may have been useful in negotiating share of the income), but later proved to be useful for Halima and her husband when they attempted to start up the shop. These small neighbourhood shops (*mudi dokhan*) depend heavily on credit and on written records.[2] It is almost unheard of for an entirely non-literate person to manage such a shop, but quite common for shop keepers to be unschooled. The shops are not great money-making enterprises, and regularly seem to fail. The shop can be viewed as a last attempt to establish and draw on relationships of credit, obligation and patronage in their community. How do we make sense of this 'return' from literacy learning? Halima was not able to improve her wellbeing. Indeed, we might say that literacy learning was correlated with a decline (negative mobility) in her economic wellbeing. However, her literacy did provide a degree of social and economic resilience (social contact, improved occupational mobility) and self-confidence that has tangible benefits.

Iqbal

Iqbal makes his living from building bamboo fences, homes and grain-stores that are used widely within north-west Bangladesh. These fences are central to the practices of purdah, encircling homesteads, and providing privacy around toilet washing areas. Most of Iqbal's work takes place within a day's travel from his home. His family own's a small homestead, with barely enough space to grow a few trees and vines. He does not earn a lot. Nevertheless, his income is partially insulated from the effects of seasonality, and benefits from storms and floods which make replacement of bamboo structures necessary. More wealthy households have corrugated tin homes (roofs first, and then walls). However, in the north-west, there is no shortage of bamboo-built homesteads. Although he is poor, the stability that his income provides is sufficient to support his family. Iqbal and his wife had no formal education. His wife is illiterate in Bangla, but reads Arabic for religious purposes which is a widespread practice amongst Bangladeshi Muslims. Two of his children are attending high school. Now in his late forties Iqbal is very physically frail. He is not able to do hard labouring work, and suffers from night blindness. I first met him in an adult literacy night class in 1997. At first I thought that he was struggling with the intellectual aspects of literacy, but later I found that poor eyesight (night-blindness) was the problem. We read during the night class by oil lamps, but in the day time he practised with the support of friends, and eventually became sufficiently competent to keep written records in his work. The records were not for the actual fence building. That is done by memory and measures using hands and arms. Paper plans are not required. However, literacy is useful for financial records associated with his work, the purchase of bamboo and tools, records of credit and debt. It was useful in his daily travel to work (often by bus), where reading bus tickets was necessary for getting a seat, and where reading road and street signs was a daily occurrence.

In many ways Iqbal's life is a story of chronic poverty. Their family has suffered numerous health-related shocks (including the death of several children), and their wellbeing is precariously dependent on his health and ability to work. They live in a tiny home and have no land. Nevertheless, they are able to support two children attending high school, and this intergenerational change may provide some longer-term financial security. One of his earliest uses of his literacy that he reported was when he checked his credit note from the local shop and found inaccuracies in the bill. He was able to ask a friend to check, and later persuaded the shop-keeper to refund the difference. Although not a huge amount, it was equal to the income from a couple of days work. For someone on the margins of wellbeing, such gains are important. For Iqbal literacy has had a significant 'return', but not one that would normally be noted by large-scale economic analysis. It also contributed to the daily physical mobility (travel, finding places of work) that was central to his livelihood. Literacy learning has contributed to his self-esteem and confidence and his new identity as a literate person has influenced his status in social encounters. It had also enabled him to improve the micro-practices of daily economic management.

Conclusions: re-thinking mobility

The concept of 'marginal returns' discussed in this paper is informed by the idea that for people experiencing the multiple constraints and vulnerabilities of chronic poverty, educational returns may be experienced as small incremental benefits rather than significant upward occupational mobility or significantly raised income. Such benefits may be modest, but can make a difference to the poor. The returns of education and learning may be experienced for example, as the ability to sustain a level of wellbeing and social standing, to make a living, manage poverty and as insurance avoid a descent into destitution (Dercon 2004; Khan and Seeley 2005). Similarly, as the examples illustrate, economic benefits of education may be outweighed (and obscured) by wider components that prevent people from escaping poverty. This is a 'return' then, but not as we know it. The vignettes also ask us to re-think the space of mobility associated with education in the context of chronic poverty. The kinds of physical mobility presented in the paper (seasonal migration, work in the local community) are not typical of the education-related movement that we might be familiar with, but are nevertheless important for the livelihoods and wellbeing of the individuals concerned. These returns may be obtained from primary schooling, or from adult literacy programmes. In the case of adult literacy, the paper suggests that care is required to conceptualise, identify and design programmes in a way that they can effectively enable such benefits, and to recognise them when they are achieved.

To capture these kinds of returns and mobility involves significant epistemological, theoretical and methodological challenges. A theory of returns to education in contexts of chronic poverty must not only recognise the effects of school attendance and completion, but also how knowledge gained in interrupted and incomplete schooling and in informal learning can impact on people's lives. An analysis and comparison of returns to education based on the attainment of formal educational qualifications and formal employment is least likely to capture such benefits. There is, however, no reason why such ethnographically derived insights should not be further explored in economics. Further work is required to develop measures that are more sensitively calibrated to the types of physical and socio-economic mobility available.

Acknowledgements
My sincere thanks to colleagues, Pieter Serneels, Edward Anderson, and Richard Palmer-Jones for their valuable comments on this paper, and the contribution of two anonymous referees.

Notes
1. My thanks to Vegard Iversen for this insight.
2. I conducted an ethnographic survey on the educational and literate status of small neighbourhood shops and their use of credit.

References
Ahmed, M., S. Nath, and K. Ahmed, eds. 2003. *Literacy in Bangladesh: Need for a new vision*. Dhaka: Campaign for Popular Education (CAMPE) and Education Watch.
Baulch, B., and P. Davis. 2008. Poverty dynamics and life trajectories in rural Bangladesh. *International Journal of Multiple Research Approaches* 2, no. 2: 176–90.
Blommaert, J. 2008. *Grassroots literacy: Writing, identity and voice in Central Africa*. London: Routledge.
Bremen, J. 1996. *Footloose labour: Working in India's informal economy*. Cambridge: Cambridge University Press.
Chronic Poverty Research Centre. 2008. *Escaping poverty traps: Annual report of the Chronic Poverty Research Group*. Manchester: Chronic Poverty Research Centre
Corbett, M. 2007. *Learning to leave: The irony of schooling in a coastal community*. Halifax, Canada: Fernwood Publishing.
Dercon, S. 2004. *Insurance against poverty*. Oxford: Oxford University Press.
Dufflo, E. 2001. Schooling and labor market consequences of school construction in Indonesia: Evidence from an unusual policy experiment. *American Economic Review* 91, no. 4: 795–813.
Glewwe, P. 2002. Schools and skills in developing countries: Education policies and socio-economic outcomes. *Journal of Economic Literature* 40, no. 2: 436–82.
Harriss-White, B. 2003. *India working: Essays on society and economy*. Cambridge: Cambridge University Press.
Hulme, D. 2004. Thinking 'small' and the understanding of poverty: Maymana and Mofizul's story. *Journal of Human Development and Capabilities* 5, no. 1: 161–76.
Hulme, D., and M. Green. 2005. From correlates and characteristics to causes: Thinking about poverty from a chronic poverty perspective. *World Development* 33: 867–79.
Hulme, D., and A. Shepherd, eds. 2003. Conceptualising chronic poverty. Special issue, *World Development* 31, no. 3.
Jeffrey, C., P. Jeffery, and R. Jeffery. 2007. *Degrees without freedom? Education, masculinities and unemployment in North India*. Stanford, CA: University of Stanford Press.
Kell, C. 1999. Teaching letters: The recontextualisation of letter writing practices in literacy classes for unschooled adults in South Africa. In *Letter writing as a social practice*, ed. D. Barton and N. Hall, 209–32. Amsterdam: John Benjamins.

Khan, I., and J. Seeley. 2005. *Making a living: The livelihoods of the rural poor in Bangladesh.* Dhaka: University Press.

Maddox, B. 2007. What can ethnographic studies tell us about the consequences of literacy. *Comparative Education* 43, no. 2: 253–71.

Maddox, B. 2008. What good is literacy? Insights and implications of the capabilities approach. *Journal of Human Development* 9, no. 2: 185–206.

Nussbaum, M. 2000. Women's capabilities and social justice. *Journal of Human Development* 1: 219–47.

Paci, P., and P. Serneels. 2007. *Employment and shared growth: Rethinking the role of labour mobility for development.* Washington, DC: World Bank.

Pritchett, L. 2001. Where has all the education gone? *The World Bank Economic Review* 15, no. 3: 367–91.

Psacharopoulos, G., and H. Patrinos. 2004. Returns to investment in education: A further update. *Education Economics* 12: 111–34.

Quisumbing, A. 2007. Poverty transitions, shocks and consumption in rural Bangladesh: Preliminary results from a longitudinal household study. Chronic Poverty Research Centre Working Paper, no. 105, Manchester.

Rahman, R.I. 2006. Access to education and employment: Implications for poverty. PRCPB Working Paper, no. 14, Programme for Research on Chronic Poverty in Bangladesh (PRCPB), Bangladesh Institute of Development Studies (BIDS), Chronic Poverty Research Centre (CPRC), and Institute for Development Policy and Management (IDPM).

Robinson-Pant, A. 2008. Why 'literacy matters': Exploring a policy perspective on literacies, identities and social change. *Journal of Development Studies* 44: 779–96.

Rose, P., and C. Dyer, 2006. Chronic poverty and education: A review of the literature. Background paper for Chronic Poverty Research Centre Report 2008–9, Chronic Poverty Research Centre, Manchester.

Save the Children. 2005. *Inheriting extreme poverty: Household aspirations, community attitudes and childhood in Northern Bangladesh.* Dhaka: Save the Children UK.

Seeley, J., B. Maddox, and M. Islam. 2006. Exploring the dynamics of extreme poverty in rural Bangladesh. Report to CARE Rural Livelihoods Programme, Dhaka, Bangladesh.

Sen, B., and D. Hulme. 2007. *The state of the poorest 2005/2006: Chronic poverty in Bangladesh – Tales of ascent, descent, marginality and persistence.* Dhaka/Manchester: Bangladesh Institute of Development Studies/CPRC/IDPM.

Street, B., ed. 1995. *Literacy and development: Ethnographic perspectives.* London: Routledge.

Trostel, M. 2005. Nonlinearity in the return to education. *Journal of Applied Economics* 8: 191–202.

Wood, G. 2003. Staying secure, staying poor: The Faustian bargain. *World Development* 31: 455–71.

Zavala, V. 2008. Mail that feeds the family. Popular correspondence and official literacy campaigns. In *Interdisciplinary approaches to literacy and development,* ed. K. Basu, B. Maddox, and A. Robinson-Pant, 880–91. London: Routledge.

Standardized individuality: cosmopolitanism and educational decision-making in an Atlantic Canadian rural community

Michael J. Corbett

School of Education, Acadia University, Wolfville, Nova Scotia, Canada

> With the rise of network society, consumerism, individualization, globalization and contemporary change forces, students are pressured to both perform well in standardized academic assessments while at the same time constructing a non-standard, unique project of the self. I argue that this generates a particular set of place-based tensions for rural students. The paper analyses data from a three-year study of youth educational decision-making to explore the tensions between place-based habitus and the mobility imperative in formal schooling.

Introduction: common sense

> Young people still grow up in rural families and go off to cities, not to return. But now it is felt that this is what they *should* do. (Berry 1990, 162, emphasis in original)

For Pierre Bourdieu school represented a space in which forms of cultural capital are acquired and negotiated in the routine practices and habits of the institution. The family, on the other hand, represents another social space with parallel processes of cultural capital acquisition, habitual practices and negotiation. What operates are more or less distinct 'markets,' i.e. the market of the family and that of the school. While Bourdieu makes no explicit distinction between urban and rural locations there is considerable space in Bourdieu's framework for developing a more nuanced sense of how cultural capital and family educational strategies work in different locales both internationally and internally across different national contexts. The spatial turn in social and educational theorizing (Usher 2002; Green and Letts 2007) would suggest that families operate in localized spaces mediated by the relative social and cultural position of parents. This social positioning then takes on different meanings as children enter school to learn the value of their family's social capital within the institution.

This study was conducted in a coastal community in Atlantic Canada. Historically the community has been relatively isolated, only getting paved road access in the mid-1950s. The community skirts two rich Atlantic bays and has a long history of inshore fishing. This fishery was transformed, beginning in the 1950s, into an industrial, year-round high-yield industry with the adoption of dragger technology and the use of larger and more powerful boats and mobile gear. The industrial fishery began to decline by the mid-1980s and since that time the industry has downsized and restructured. As a consequence, this community has experienced considerable depopulation within the last 30 years. The general pattern is not unlike that found in many rural and coastal communities in North America which transformed from multi-occupational resource extraction economies to relatively exclusive, single primary resource industries, and ultimately to ecologically and economically challenged post-industrial rural places.

The establishment of secondary schooling in the community as a normal part of the life course is a relatively new phenomenon, really only getting established in the 1970s for girls and in the 1990s for boys (Corbett 2001). Many current high school students are the first generation of high school graduates in their families. Many families have relied more on extensive networks of family and neighborly connection than on the formal credentials of the education system. Historically people in the villages have prided themselves in an unschooled acumen, practicality, multi-skilled laboring adaptability, toughness, and hard work. This 'down home' common-sense represents a set of life practices that worked for generations that have both exploited and tried to defend one of the richest and most diverse fisheries in the world. An embattled sense of persistence and a survivalist cunning marks the character of many successful fishing families in this community. On the other hand, within institutions of formal education and elite rural families, discourses of academic engagement, mobility and escaping the community have become important markers of educational and social privilege (Corbett 2007a; Carr and Kefalas 2009; Holdsworth 2009).

In many ways the institutional practices of the school and the kinds of people who work there are contrasted with the toughness and independence of fishing people. This has created ambivalence and resistance to school and schooling. It has also led to a more or less radical separation between Bourdieu's two 'markets,' which have tended to have little positive or mutually supportive contact. With very few exceptions, one either integrated into the local and its apprenticeship-style informal education system, or one left the community often using formal education to make the break.

As sociologists as diverse as Corbett (2007a), Palsson (1994, 1999), Rose (2004), and Smyth and Hattam (2005) have shown, the ordinary business of living a working-class life requires considerable cognitive and physical skill. What studies like these point toward is the well-known sociological 'black box' of the school tends to reproduce predictable social class-based academic results. This is in part because 'nonacademic' youth have options and choose their way out of lifestyles and career trajectories promoted in formal education (Lehmann 2007 ; Corbett 2007a; Smyth and Hattam 2004). So rather than the interpolation of subjects into particular social class positions through the exercise of centralized institutional power, it is actually in skilled accomplishments and situated learning (Wenger 1998; Palsson 1994, 1999) that students establish 'non-academic' identities. As one student put it:

> You know I try, but I'm just not a school person. I don't really understand most of it, like English and math. I'll get through it, I have to. I like doing things with my hands, you know, where you see what you're doing and you can take pride in it. (Male student 1W, aged 15)

In rural North American contexts, there are few qualitative analyses of rural education. It is interesting that while the predominantly urban-centric sociology of education has focused heavily on the social mobility of youth, the rural sociology of education has tended to focus on the geographic mobility of youth, typically away from rural areas. Indeed there have been a number of studies of youth migration from rural parts of North America exclusively focused on national or regional data sets. There has been relatively little work done on rurality and identity or qualitative studies in rural education.

In Europe there have been a number of analyses which use qualitative methods to understand the connection between geographic and social mobility as well as the different tensions involved in the development of educational and occupational trajectories for rural youth (Baeck 2004; Bjarnason and Thorlindsson 2006; Jamieson 2000; Jones 1995, 1999; Ní Laoire 2000, 2005; Reed Danahay 1997; Stockdale 2002; Wiborg 2001). All of these studies demonstrate in somewhat different ways that the journey through school for rural youth is inundated with a set of problems concerning geographic mobility not ordinarily faced by urban youth who can pursue postsecondary education close to home. The distinction between the perceived excitement in urban spaces and the safe, yet boring world of a rural home community typically fuels a strong desire amongst youth for outmigration. At the same time discourses of rural decline and depopulation cause tension around what is seen as a brain drain (Carr and Kefalas 2009). Additionally, home places tend to be difficult to leave for a variety of reasons having to do with both positive attachments and obligations, on the one hand, and powerful obstacles to leaving on the other.

This study uses ethnographic observation and semi-structured interviews in order to understand how young people in a Canadian coastal community manage the tension between learning and leaving. The study, entitled *Where I Belong*, draws on a six-month period of ethnography, a series of 11 semi-structured parental interviews, and 60 semi-structured interviews with 20 youth between the ages of 13 and 18 attending a regional secondary high school in a rural community in Atlantic Canada. The fieldwork and interviews were conducted between October 2004 and June 2007 by the principal investigator and three graduate research assistants in the regional secondary school. The sample comprised 20 of 21 students from a coastal community attending a regional secondary school some 15–35 km from the youth's home villages. Parents were chosen at random and represented 55% of the student sample. Parents were interviewed by the principal investigator in their own homes, and in one case, in a restaurant.

Where I Belong attempts to understand the importance of place to youth raised in rural coastal communities which have historically relied on the small-boat Atlantic fishery but which have undergone significant 'restructuring' in recent decades due to technological change, global capitalism and the rise of network society among other factors. This restructuring and its impact on educational decision-making in the lives of community residents was the subject of a previous study entitled *Learning to Leave* (Corbett 2001, 2004, 2005, 2007a). This earlier study analyzed the career and educational trajectories of more than 700 people who grew up in this coastal community from the late 1950s to the late 1990s. *Where I Belong* takes this analysis further to look at the process of educational decision-making in this community under current conditions. All quotes in this paper are take from interviews and fieldwork associated with the *Where I Belong* project.

Where I Belong is interested in the way that parents and youth themselves understand and construct their understandings of local places and spaces. The central research question in this study concerns how youth and their parents conceptualize: (1) their local communities and (2) their maturation into this rural coastal community as young adults, or alternatively, their trajectories away from this community through formal education or other mobilities. Specifically I am interested in the ways in which families seek to transform capital which has its primary value in localized markets into the more widely negotiable capital that schools can help build (i.e. credentials). Increasingly the 'market of the school' is the principal means through which most youth accumulate cultural capital.

Floating in space: discussion of findings

A number of commentators have written in recent years about how educational thought has been slow to incorporate ideas of space and place (Usher 2002; Green and Letts 2007). Historically, schools have promoted both a vision of liberal individualism (Theobald 1997; Bowers 2006), and a corollary notion of uniform provision (Green and Letts 2007) of educational opportunities to all citizens. As such, problems of educational governance and provision have been constructed as a temporal movement of practice and outcomes away from exclusive place-based traditions toward allegedly inclusive and egalitarian visions of the individual freed from constraint. In this view, place is either viewed as a neutral 'container' for action or the problem that education solves. Places represent attachments to the particular, to established alliances, and to local loyalties which modern educational systems supplant with broader regional, national and even international allegiances.

Giddens (1979, 1981) describes the way that advanced societies also overcome the limitations of space through the application of various technologies of control. These technologies have had the effect of 'disembedding' citizens from particular locales, effectively setting us loose in a world dominated by expert systems, professionals, impersonal symbolic token exchanges (money is the most obvious example), all of which both assuage and generate insecurity at the same time. The work is done not so much by multi-skilled bricoleurs (which is often the locally understood view of an intelligent person in my study community), but by 'experts' whose work is unseen and not well understood locally.

Institutional schooling can be understood in this way as a disembedding mechanism (Giddens 1990). In rural and other isolated areas it also takes on an additional role in support of geographic mobility. Of course, this physical mobility is supported by other ways of loosening attachment to local places and spaces. For instance, curriculum develops through the grade levels, the work and content become more abstract, theoretical and more detached from place. Indeed, in the classic formulation of Piaget, cognitive development is understood as a linear path from the concrete and the immediate, to the abstract and the theoretical. Durkheim's (1956) classic work on schooling similarly focuses on the transcendence of a concrete place-based mechanical solidarity for an organic solidarity focused on complex and distantiated social relationships. The market of the school represents the abstract and interconnected modern 'expert system' (Giddens 1990), while the market of the family represents tangible face-to-face attachments. The entire enterprise from the work of nineteenth-century school promoters, to contemporary educational reformers, has been a protracted engagement with moving young people out of the specificity of their 'places' into the universality of the created spaces in industrial and post-industrial capitalism (Lefebvre 1991). In the context of rural communities, this movement away from place and into larger space involves a geographic trajectory away from kinship networks, villages, and small towns. More precisely perhaps, contemporary change forces, networks of information, trade, and human mobility have now pervaded all aspects of life in North American rural communities, changing the way that place is understood and experienced, particularly by youth.

Indeed it is one role of the rural school to insure that these contemporary spaces, many of them virtual, come to infuse the lives of children and youth living in relatively isolated places. The mobile imagery associated with rural schooling is instantiated in a complex of routine practices which privilege and valorize an exodus from the locale (Corbett 2006; Carr and Kefalas 2009). I begin this analysis with a look at the spatial practices involved in a rural high school graduation. I then go on to look at changes in the timing of key adolescent/emergent adult status passages and differences in temporal norms around these passages. Finally, I look at the particular challenges youth in this community face accomplishing identity work which both meets institutional standards and still represents a unique but credible life-project orientation.

Parallel graduation celebrations

As Popkewitz (1998) argues, rural places are melded with the other quintessential problem spaces of contemporary capitalism (i.e. the inner city) to represent 'broken' places that routinely produce and reproduce academic failure. In the way that place is invoked in this discourse, children are presented not so much as underperforming students as victims of places so damaged that they could only produce substandard results and fail to integrate into the standardized educational dreamscapes. Marginal urban/rural places themselves have failed and the only educational hope is that through education some subset of youth living in them can be taught to save themselves and learn to leave (Corbett 2007a; Kelly 2009).

In rural education this mobility imperative creates a number of interesting educational dynamics. These include: (1) implicit and explicit messages about rurality in the curriculum; (2) the relevance of curriculum to those students who are not on the 'leaving' track; (3) the image of the 'successful' mobile student and the unsuccessful 'stuck' other; (4) the ambivalent connection between community/place and curriculum; and (5) the idea of schooling as the acquisition of capital that may be negotiable in metropolitan spaces. The problem of youth outmigration and brain drain is juxtaposed in tension with the concern for those children who do not leave, generating a kind of Catch-22 for communities that ironically find themselves celebrating the loss of human resources to cities and large towns.

The ambivalence and ceremony surrounding rural high school graduation activities and ceremonies is instructive here and I want to begin with an analysis of a student assistant's field notes from an ethnographic study of the end of the school year in a rural high school. The graduation celebration in North American rural communities is the punctuation mark which has traditionally celebrated the acquisition of a high-status 'ticket' to leave. These ceremonies tend to celebrate those students whose educational trajectory is likely to take them farthest from home:

> Students who are 'just graduating' without honours or scholarships are shuffled across the stage with a smile and a quick handshake. For them graduation takes but a few seconds. Where do they go after this event? Students who graduate with honours on the other hand, stand while their accomplishments, awards and scholarships are announced ... there is no question that this ceremony is a door to more education and other places. (Field notes from high school graduation ceremony, June 2005)

Families are positioned in these graduation ceremonies as the institutional remnant of community, a space which is expected to be left behind. Parents sit in their seats and listen. It is all about going somewhere and 'moving on'.

Formal celebrations around graduation are only part of the process. Family gatherings can themselves be elaborate given that many of the graduates are the first in their families to have achieved a high school diploma. Indeed the entire process consumes nearly a week of celebration including the graduation ceremony itself, a formal graduation dance called the prom,[1] family events, an organized alcohol-free 'safe grad party,' and various informal 'grad parties.' Each of these events provides opportunity to mark the break with community represented by graduation. The most important status event for the students themselves is the prom which, through an affectation of elegance, represents the antithesis of the rural place. The prom not only provides an opportunity for outwardly mobile, academically successful, 'popular' grads to display family wealth, it is also an entry into an exciting, hyper-urban space:

> One group of popular girls turned up in a limo with their older dates ... I then saw another limo pull up and a horse drawn carriage and then an old fashioned horse drawn buggy. Inside the school they had done a wonderful job in creating a Hollywood scene. On the bleachers were the Hollywood Hills and around the room were scattered several palm trees, while the walls were covered in movie posters and old records. (Field notes, prom, 2005)

All of this display demonstrates how the graduate is leaving the community behind and has few ongoing attachments with the place. Invocation of Hollywood which is the quintessential dream-place adds to the effect. But not all students are on the leaving track.

At an informal graduation party the separation of mobile, 'popular' graduates was also evident. This event, held in an isolated gravel pit, was mainly attended by less mobile graduates, younger high school students, and by adults in the community. The party featured loud music, excessive drinking, hyper-masculine displays including fighting and motorized four-wheeler tricks, and young adults 'checking out' high school students. This party appeared to be little different from a more ordinary bush party but it was presented as an informal graduation event. The field worker who observed the event was surprised by many things including the virtual absence of one subset of the graduates at the party, the 'popular' youth:

> As the night wore on more older people began to show up. There were a lot of older men and some women at the party. Some came to the party on foot and others came on 4-wheelers (small all terrain vehicles). The grade 12 popular girls and their boyfriends, who had all graduated a couple of years before had planned a camping trip to local campground for the night. However, they did decide to show up at the grad party for about half an hour in their sweat shirts and ball caps with ponytails hanging out the back. (Field notes, informal grad party, 2005)

Unlike the formal graduation events, this party was more about integration into the local community through a set of adult social practices as well as displays of masculinity and femininity.[2] In other words, it seems to have functioned as an alternative graduation, or as a celebration of the integration of non-graduates or locally-oriented graduates into the locale. It was more about moving in than moving on. The informal party had little to do with graduation and a great deal more to do with the reproduction of local social class practices around femininity and masculinity, bush culture and local mobility represented by the four-wheeler, drug use, and sexuality. The heteronormative gender positioning of young men and women as well as age difference seems to demonstrate traditions of local conjugal reproduction and early initiation of youth into the community habitus of adult work and play. The 'popular' youth who make a brief appearance have all established relationships with people who had either graduated and left the community previously, or who were 'from' another locale. These youth are essentially in transit.

The vignette also illustrates the power of the 'party scene' to seduce and integrate young people. It is a socialization event in which familiar social practices and local social space are celebrated, contrasting the celebration of formal credentialing and leaving embedded in the official graduation and the prom. In a social milieu in which 'growing up early' has historically been seen as a sign of maturity and as a way of entering into an intense adult culture of hard work, hegemonic masculinity, desirable femininity, and access to resources:

> I think it's just a lot of pressure; they take it just so hard ... and when they get pressure squeezed by their peers they just seem to cave in. They start so young. And if the guy next door is going to drink on the weekend, you know, well you've got to too, and the guy next door to him has to, and the guy next to you has to. They all have to think it's a great big deal running and rampaging the neighborhood trying to find the next best thing that's going to happen. And it's such a shame to see the young people thinking that's all they have to look forward to. That's being a real man. (Female parent 1R)

Intensity of local attachments is demonstrated in school in singular attachment to local cliques or identity positions. These youth are attached to the mythology of a working fishery in which physical toughness and stamina are valued and valuable. For concerned parents, youth is understood as a mine-field of seductions including early engagement in adult pleasures like alcohol, drugs and sexual activity. They worry about their children 'falling in' to adult-like social behavior while they are still children, yet at the same time they encourage independence and early adult-like engagement in local work sites. A common view was expressed by this parent who said, 'They gotta learn to get to work and that nothing comes to you for nothing. You learn that out workin' not in school and it ain't ever too early to get the message' (Male parent 1N).

For youth, the seductions are well understood and often articulated as a kind of trap sprung in the form of a love affair or being blind-sided by drugs and alcohol. Spatially, these practices are understood as the chains that can tie an individual to the place and render education impossible or irrelevant:

> My friend ... I always thought she was going to be like a doctor because she was the type of girl that she could read something and remember it ... but lately she's been ... she's had a boyfriend for a long time now ... she wanted to be a doctor, she wanted to be a pharmacist and ... and actually she just dropped math 12 advanced ... she thought it was too much. Her boyfriend is 22 I think and so he's out of school and he's already settled down ... and things like that and he also parties a lot. I think he wants her with him all the time. (Female student 1L)

Yet the hard-working, hard-drinking culture remains alive if not vital. Most youth survive and in the process many also develop a complex of life skills and networks in a DIY culture of renovation, repair, networking, periodic work, state transfers and family land ownership. This nonacademic cultural and social capital can provide a precarious but familiar living.

Timing and pressure to grow up

Taking things seriously, 'deferring gratification' and working hard in school where the immediate relevance of what is happening is not always evident have been chief attitudinal markers associated with the middle classes. In many respects learning to leave spaces of the practical and to embrace irrelevance is the marker of academic success. By 'embracing irrelevance' I mean the process in which some working-class families that have little experience and/or success in secondary and postsecondary education manage to bracket their mistrust of the apparent impracticality and irrelevance of academic work and encourage their children to take it seriously. In other words, what needs to be deferred is not 'gratification' but an immediate pay-cheque and the pragmatic rigors of adult life. This typically involves a relatively radical shift in thinking about what knowledge is worthwhile, setting aside valued local knowledge which is immediately relevant and practical in favor of high-status academic knowledge which has little immediate local application (e.g. literature, higher maths, theoretical physics and chemistry).

Embracing irrelevance and discouraging early immersion in adult social and work practices are key facets of a larger set of practices that professional educators typically judge as 'involved parenting'. Lareau (2003) calls this configuration of social practices, 'concerted cultivation' involving both a roster of high-status, individuated, parent-organized extra-curricular activities as well as the modeling and inculcation of a critical attitude toward institutional actors like teachers. 'Involved parenting' has tended to be defined by many Western educators as a process in which parents actively help their children navigate institutions and activities that position youth for postsecondary education. This, however, is changing as postsecondary education becomes ubiquitous, not only amongst the middle classes, but also in what are called non-traditional postsecondary families, including those living in marginal and isolated places where the economic opportunity to 'drop out' and access low-skill employment is in decline. More and more, those youth whose families counted on their attachment to place, land ownership, kinship and friendship networks (social capital), access to natural resources and exclusive harvesting privileges (e.g. commercial fishing licenses, gear/equipment, know-how, etc.) have been forced to engage in institutions of formal education for the first time.

Orienting offspring in postsecondary education is now understood by most families as a 'necessity' or at least as a 'safe' course compared to the rough and ready alternative of boom-and-bust 'oil patch' work in western Canada or precarious employment prospects at home. The challenge in many families is to find a justification for opportunity costs and the large amounts of time apparently wasted 'just sitting' in school. For families whose experience with postsecondary education is limited, the long-term advantage of the investment is not yet established notwithstanding college and university outreach programs targeting non-traditional families:

> You have to be smart about taking the right program. There are too many of them down here that went off someplace to take some course and who end up back here with nothing. If you get in the wrong thing and there's no jobs, well you're out of luck. Them Arts degrees is a good example. They don't seem to lead to anything unless you're going into

teaching. Well, there's some teaching jobs, but not everyone can be a teacher. (Male parent 2L)

At the same time a considerable literature is emerging which deals with the way that contemporary youth are making nonstandard transitions through the normative markers that signal adulthood. The 'emergent adult' (Arnett 2004) literature has argued that the transition from school to work to school occurs in different combinations and timing sequences is becoming highly variable. Yet the idea of variability of trajectories seems to miss the possibility that for some youth the 'correct' timing of life events may continue to be important and highly structured. The loosely structured, exploratory framework which characterizes the notion of emerging adulthood with its identity fixation, educational side-roads, experimental relationships, and boomerang residential patterns in and out of the parental home is not universally available. In fact, such loose trajectories require considerable family resources.

My data suggest that in families which have not had significant historical postsecondary experience, higher education is typically understood in highly pragmatic, job-oriented terms. In other words, these families are no longer 'disengaged' from their children's schooling, leaving key educational decisions to school personnel (Lareau 2003). Locally integrated families, however, continue to think of their children's future in terms of staying rather than leaving the community:

Like he's going to college and I think most of them are. There ain't much choice today. If they take the right training for this area, for what jobs there is around here, they'll do all right. Like being a carpenter for instance, or accounting, or bookkeeping. He could train to work in banks. There's a number of different things that you could probably train for, and possibly, potentially get a job here. You know, as the population gets older there's people who has them jobs now; there's people who are retiring all the time. (Male parent 1T)

Yet the pressure to choose and choose correctly creates its own set of problems and tensions:

Mom and dad told me I could go to college but they said I only got one shot. You know, I couldn't frig around, I had to know what I wanted. Well, I don't know what I want. It's a lot of pressure. Me and my friends ... some of us anyway, we're gonna stay around here for awhile till we decide. You know, work and save some money. (Male student 4C, aged 17)

So an important question is the extent to which pressure in more economically challenged, nontraditional postsecondary families to get the big decisions right often leads to not making them at all. In other words, by doing exactly what teachers and school people have goaded working-class families to do for so long (i.e. to take the process seriously and engage with children in educational decision-making), are these families inadvertently diverting their own children away from high-status forms of postsecondary participation? Fear of making the wrong high-stakes decision both speeds up the pace of timing for crucial transitions and forces youth to make tough, complex decisions quickly or alternatively to defer and wait. On the other hand, more privileged peers are encouraged to make such decisions slowly and after a process of protracted identity exploration. Youth from 'practical' families define themselves as the kind of people who do not waste time and who always take the efficient route.

> I don't know ... um mom had hoped that I'd go to Dal or something and so like engineering ... for like ...whether it would be for designing and buildings or cars or stuff like that...um because I took physics awhile back and Mr. XXXX said that it was something he could see me doing ... architecture or something like that ... engineering ... like I thought about that. I got a program for the university, but that's a long haul. It's two years at NSCC [community college] and then you get two years of experience and then you can write your exams. (Male student 1C, aged 16)

The space afforded a young person to 'grow up' and to explore identity is differentially distributed in this study group. This is occurring at a time when it is become increasingly incumbent upon students to develop individualized life plans and choice paths. This individualized 'search for self' or development of a coherent and legitimate 'project of the self' (Giddens 1990, 1991) in the post-traditional lifeworld of contemporary capitalism is part of the general expectation of schooling today. It is also formalized through the resume and processes of portfolio construction that are part of curriculum and assessment in most parts of North America as early as junior high school. The construction of a life on paper in the proto-CV or educational portfolio is presented to youth as a choice, but increasingly it is a prerequisite for high-status scholarships, awards, and entrance to postsecondary education. These credentials, awards and experiences all ease the transition from known spaces and places in the market of the family and the opportunities, apprenticeships and forms of capital available there. The cultural capital represented in the proto-CV privileges those young people who are not forced to grow up quickly and who have space in their lives for sports, lessons, cultural activities, travel, volunteering and other forms of concerted cultivation. This is the extracurricular face of the 'floater' identity (Corbett 2007b), the engagement in resume-building adult-organized formal or semi-formal activities that generate experience and valuable cultural capital. Young people are expected to perform and meet standards, but they are also expected to construct an 'engaged' middle class self.

Standardized individuality: constructing a cosmopolitan identity

With the rise of consumerism and individualization (Giddens 1990; Bauman 2001, 2004), psychological discourses like that of emerging adulthood have been employed in recent years to frame a new stage in the life course, one that follows the well-established buffer space of adolescence (Arnett 2004; Cote 2005; Gaudet 2007; Molgat 2007). This new stage carries with it new norms and expectations which include both an increasingly nonstandard transition between school and work as well as increasing pressure to extend formal education well beyond secondary school. In emerging adulthood, which is generally defined as beginning at age 17 (the end of compulsory schooling in most western jurisdictions) and ending somewhere between age 24 and 30, the claim is that young adults do protracted identity work.[3] The point is that not everyone has the privilege of the examined life, or at least the particular form of the examined life that looks good on a CV. Transitions from school to work and toward established markers of adulthood like conjugal relations, independent living, and steady full-time employment are now said to require flexible exploration, self-examination, and experimentation.

Research in emerging adulthood essentially provides a social psychology which parallels the more individualistically pitched sociological work of contemporary theorists like Giddens, Beck, and many others. As traditional life markers and norms are swept away by the rising tide of late modernity, identity construction becomes both crucial and creative lifework for those immediately beyond the secondary school years. At the same time this new life phase is an ambivalent space in which relatively anomic young adults must make sense of complex and often confusing choices and uncharted trajectories into the supposed stability of full-fledged adult life. In fact, identity is now less about achieving stability in Erikson's original (1968) sense of the word, than it is an ongoing and endless round of self-creation, reflection, re-creation and choice (Bauman 1999).

The construction of a legitimate and flexible life project is both a descriptive and a prescriptive phenomenon. The emergent adulthood literature demonstrates its increasing commonality while the way that postsecondary institutions and youth themselves embrace portfolio assessment and CV-building experiences like international travel and personalized volunteer engagements illustrates the importance of uniqueness and commitment. At the same time these kinds of engagements are effectively valorized as acts of virtues and indicators of caring and commitment.

The planning and exploration phase in a contemporary middle-class life which is considered by powerful institutional agents and ordinary citizens alike to be 'successful,' begins earlier and carries on longer than ever before. In most Western families, life paths are no longer determined by tradition or by following well-worn pathways. A contemporary life is a 'project' (Giddens 1990; Beck 1992), a uncertain and uncharted set of linked engagements that develop into a narrative of purpose which is typically captured in one of the central pieces of personal documentation and self-promotion represented by the CV. Increasingly, the standardized accountability measures allegedly used for educational quality control are supplemented by individualized instruments of literate and ethical self-construction and self-promotion to audiences of strangers. This 'designer' addendum to the strictly timed and tested, age-stage forms of educational accountability raise the stakes in the educational game beyond quantitative standard academic performance indicators and formalize the play of cultural capital in developing an educational trajectory:

> Last year I realized that I wasn't going to university. I'm just not ... I'm not into the same things as the girls who are going there. You know ... I just don't like them and their preppy ... They're so perfect and they seem to think there's all the time in the world. Well the course I'm taking next year ... it's considered two years but it's only 13 months ... cause you work through the summer and everything ... and after that I think I'm just going to move back home and work for a couple of years and get some of my student loan paid off a little bit ... probably a couple of years after I graduate from XXXX [private college]. (Female student 2L, aged 17)

This transition has a particular set of effects in a rural place. Many families in this community have been challenged economically and otherwise by the corporatization and downsizing of the fishery. Those who remain are the 'survivors' who have been able to combine a range of different kinds of resources and strategies. Social and cultural capital in these families has typically positioned higher education as an esoteric and impractical and essentially arbitrary credentialing system, useful elsewhere but not locally. Yet, today, as one parent put it: 'You need a God-Damn university degree to put a nut on a bolt or sweep a floor. What smart university boys dreamed all this up?'

The whole business is typically read as a conspiracy of irrelevance and credentialing designed ultimately to drive people out of rural places. The pressure is exerted on youth by families who can no longer 'dwell in place' and for whom 'floating' in new spaces is relatively new. What is not new is that economic resources still matter. What money buys is not so much access to institutions of higher learning as the time to explore and the option to choose the 'irrelevance' of its most exclusive forms. To have the family support/resources to experience and perhaps undergo an extended 'emergent adulthood,' to explore, to experiment, to 'do anything you want' or to 'go anywhere you want' is the privilege of a relatively small cadre of youth in this community:

> I don't really feel any pressure in school at all. It's easy really. Sometimes I study with my friends. We're all good students and we're kind of against each other for the top marks. My friends are all in town and mom and dad let me use the car so, you know ... I'm in control ... that's what I mean when I say there isn't much pressure on me. If I'm somewhere I don't want to be, then I just leave. And they [parents] don't have to run me up to sports and after-school stuff so that makes it easier for them. (Female student 1M, aged 17)

That it is precisely this wide exploratory frame (including the spatial mobility afforded and symbolized in a North American rural community by a car) that allows a student to generate a valuable portfolio of activities that can demonstrate engagement and the beginnings of the middle-class trajectory that is valued in high-status postsecondary institutions.

For others, the prospect of higher education, though available and necessary, is another piece of a compulsory education that already seems too long. The problem of pressure and time limitations are the focus here. And it is an ambivalence about the value of the educational engagement as well as the importance of choosing 'correctly' within a restricted time frame, and finding both what you want to do and something for which there is a labour market constraint and sometimes actually inhibits the choice of non-privileged youth:

> I find they [parents] put a lot of pressure on me ... it could be just because we don't have money to do what we need to do ... and so I think that puts a lot of pressure on them too ... that's what makes me feel a little edgy too [sigh] ... because where the two of them are working and where they feel like they're under a lot of pressure that makes me feel like well how am I going to do when I get out? I'd hate to start off by getting a student loan that I'm going to have to start paying on as soon as I'm done school ... I don't want to do that ... that's the reason why I'm deciding whether or not I'm going to go or not. A lot of people when they go and take five years for something later on they just end up working in a restaurant ... a lot of people who get student loans they just get it for nothing. (Male student 3L, aged 16)

Even if this young man can manage to keep his marks up to compete with the young woman quoted above, their lifestyles and the spaces they inhabit make it unlikely that he will build the kind of 'portfolio' of academic achievement, strong standardized test scores and CV-building voluntary engagements that will allow him to see himself as competitive and begin the process of leaving the known.

Conclusion

The market of the school has now been transformed. It demands a safe passage through the trials and temptations of the adult work/party scene. The traditional life path of early immersion in adulthood remains a powerful identity hook for many youth. This is combined with and set against new demands around the allegedly objective standards represented by standardized tests and school grades and also by the nuanced and subtle business of constructing a credible and rich project of the self.

Finally, and perhaps most importantly, youth and their families are challenged to break with tradition and established ideas of common-sense 'hands-on' work and accept the apparent irrelevance of academic work. This calculus for distinguishing between what is and what is not relevant and important remains, as Bourdieu (1984) demonstrated, the ultimate means of social class reproduction. Cutting out a space for exploration of what may seem immediately irrelevant appears to be the most powerful distinction between those families who are able to launch their children into high-status postsecondary engagements necessary for professional careers.

Today rural North American youth are expected to meet standards and appear unique at the same time. I have found an unequal distribution of family resources and time required to grow and explore and to establish the forms of cultural capital that ultimately allow them to do the complex symbolic work demanded in emerging post-industrial economies. This is the sometimes contradictory and highly challenging world of standardized individuality. And it is an educational space that excludes many locally-focused, 'practical', 'hands-on' youth whose lifeworlds provide a preparation for a different market, the market of the family in an increasingly challenged locale. It is the flexible, border-crossing, relaxed 'floater' who seems to be making the transition more readily than the embedded, serious 'hard core' youth intent on immediately reproducing established and visible forms of adulthood.

Ironically, those in a position to play with time, space and identity seem to satisfy the requirements of formal schooling than those youth forced early into the high-stakes business of choosing a life course decisively and choosing well. After all it is the common-sense thing to do for those driven to be practical. Freedom from early high-stakes decision-making has often been a marker of privilege. The freedom of the disembedded, free-floating exploratory 'emergent adult' is no longer cast as frivolity and irresponsibility; rather, it is formalized in terms of diverse educational experience and recast in routine educational discourse as individual accomplishment and family virtue.

Acknowledgement
The author would like to acknowledge the support of the Social Sciences and Humanities Research Council of Canada for funding the research upon which this article is based.

Notes
1. The prom is an annual graduation dance. It has become a highly formal event in recent years and in this particular community it is part of a series of ceremonies and informal events spanning the week around the official school graduation ceremony. Students typically dress in tuxedos and evening dresses and often rent limousines and even horse-drawn carriages for this event.
2. In more recent years these graduation parties are even more heavily attended because of the connections and information flows made possible by social networking websites.
3. 'Nice work if you can get it,' as the old jazz standard reminds us. Apart from critical scholarship in the sociology of education and in educational research more generally, the lie of free choice is also the subject matter of a considerable body of creative output in contemporary popular culture both in the West and globally.

References

Arnett, J. 2004. *Emerging adulthood: The winding road from the late teens through the twenties.* New York: Oxford University Press.
Baeck, D. 2004. The urban ethos: Locality and youth in north Norway. *Young* 12, no. 2: 99–115.
Bauman, Z. 1999. *In search of politics.* Stanford, CA: Stanford University Press.
Bauman, Z. 2001. *The individualized society.* Cambridge: Polity Press.
Bauman, Z. 2004. *Wasted lives: Modernity and its outcasts.* Cambridge: Polity Press.
Beck, U. 1992. *Risk society: Towards a new modernity.* London: Sage.
Berry, W. 1990. *What are people for?* New York: North Point Press.
Bjarnason T., and T. Thorlindsson. 2006. Should I stay or should I go? Migration expectations among youth in Icelandic fishing and farming communities. *Journal of Rural Studies* 22: 290–300.
Bourdieu, P. 1984. *Distinction: A social critique of the judgement of taste.* Cambridge, MA: Harvard University Press.
Bourdieu, P. 1990. *The logic of practice.* Stanford, CA: Stanford University Press.
Bowers, C. 2006. *Revitalizing the commons: Cultural and educational sites of resistance and affirmation.* Lanham MD: Rowman and Littlefield.
Carr, P., and M. Kefalas. 2009. *Hollowing out the middle: The rural brain drain and what it means for America.* Boston: Beacon Press.
Corbett, M. 2001. A protracted struggle: Rural resistance and normalization in Canadian educational history. *Historical Studies in Education* 13, no. 1: 19–48.
Corbett, M. 2004. It was fine, if you wanted to leave: Narratives of educational ambivalence from Nova Scotian coastal community 1963–1998. *Anthropology and Education* 35, no. 4: 451–71.
Corbett, M. 2005. Rural education and out-migration: The case of a coastal community. *Canadian Journal of Education* 28, nos. 1 and 2: 52–72.
Corbett, M. 2006. Educating the country out of the child and educating the child out of the country. *Alberta Journal of Educational Research* 52: 286–98.
Corbett, M. 2007a. *Learning to leave: The irony of schooling in a coastal community.* Halifax, Canada: Fernwood Press.
Corbett, M. 2007b. Learning and dreaming in space and place: Identity and rural schooling. *Canadian Journal of Education* 30, no. 3: 771–92.
Cote, J. 2005. Emerging adulthood as an institutionalized moratorium: Risks and benefits to identity formation. In *Emerging adults in America: Coming of age in the 21st century,* ed. J. Arnett and J. Tanner, 85–116. Washington, DC: American Psychological Association.
Durkheim, E. 1956. *Education and sociology.* S. Fox trans. New York: The Free Press.
Erikson, E. 1968. *Identity: Youth and crisis.* New York: Norton.
Gaudet, S. 2007. *Emerging adulthood: A new stage in the life course.* PRI Project – Investing in Youth. Ottawa: Government of Canada.
Giddens, A. 1979. *Central problems in social theory: Action, structure and contradiction in social analysis.* London: Macmillan.
Giddens, A. 1981. *A contemporary critique of historical materialism.* Berkeley and Los Angeles: University of California Press.
Giddens, A. 1990. *The consequences of modernity.* Stanford, CA: Stanford University Press.
Giddens, A. 1991. *Modernity and self-identity: Self and society in the late modern age.* Stanford, CA: Stanford University Press.
Green, B., and W. Letts. 2007. Space, equity and rural education: A 'trialectical' account. In *Spatial theories of education: Policy and geography matters,* ed. K. Gulson and C. Symes, 57–76. London and New York: Routledge.
Holdsworth, C. 2009. 'Going away to uni': Mobility, modernity, and independence of English higher education students. *Environment and Planning* 41, no. 8: 1849–64.
Jamieson, L. 2000. Migration, place and class: Youth in a rural area. *The Sociological Review* 48: 203–23.
Jones, G. 1995. *Leaving home.* Buckingham, UK: Open University Press.
Jones, G. 1999. Trail blazers and path followers: Social reproduction and geographic mobility in youth. In *The myth of intergenerational conflict: The family and the state in ageing societies,* ed. S. Arber and C. Attias-Donfut, 154–73. London and New York: Routledge.

Kelly, U. 2009. *Migration and education in a multicultural world: Culture, loss, and identity.* New York: Palgrave Macmillan.

Lareau, A. 2003. *Unequal childhoods: Class, race and family life.* Berkeley: University of California Press.

Lefebvre, H. 1991. *The production of space.* Cambridge: Basil Blackwell.

Lehmann, W. 1997. *Choosing to labour: School-work transitions and social class.* Montreal & Kingston: McGill Queens University.

Molgat, M. 2007. Do transitions and social structures matter? How 'emerging adults' define themselves as adults. *Journal of Youth Studies* 10: 495–516.

Ní Laoire, C. 2000. Conceptualising Irish rural youth migration: A biographical approach. *International Journal of Population Geography* 6: 229–43.

Ní Laoire, C. 2005. 'You're not a man at all!': Masculinity, responsibility, and staying on the land in contemporary Ireland. *Irish Journal of Sociology* 14, no. 2: 94–114.

Palsson, G. 1994. Enskilment at sea. *Man* 29: 901–27.

Palsson, G. 1999. Schooling and skipperhood: The development of dexterity. *American Anthropologist* 100: 908–23.

Popkewitz, T. 1998. *Struggling for the soul: The politics of schooling and the construction of the teacher.* New York: Teachers College Press.

Reed-Danahay, D. 1997. *Education and identity in rural France: The politics of schooling.* Cambridge: Cambridge University Press.

Rose, M. 2004. *The mind at work: Valuing the intelligence of the American worker.* New York: Penguin.

Smyth, J., and R. Hattam. 2004. *Dropping out, drifting off, being excluded: Becoming somebody without school.* New York: Peter Lang.

Stockdale, A. 2002. Out-migration from rural Scotland: The importance of family and social networks. *Sociologia Ruralis* 42, no. 1: 41–64.

Theobald, P. 1997. *Teaching the commons: Place, pride and the renewal of community.* Boulder, CO: Westview Press.

Usher, R. 2002. Putting space back on the map: Globalisation, place and identity. *Educational Philosophy and Theory* 34: 41–55.

Wenger, E. 1998. *Communities of practice: Learning, meaning and identity.* Cambridge: Cambridge University Press.

Wiborg, A. 2001. Education, mobility and ambivalence: Rural students in higher education. *Young* 9: 23–40.

Whose education? The inclusion of Gypsy/Travellers: continuing culture and tradition through the right to choose educational opportunities to support their social and economic mobility

Christine O'Hanlon

CARE/EDU, University of East Anglia, Norwich, UK

> Traveller education takes place through family and community life regardless of formal school input. This paper defines the benefits or otherwise of education to support the social and economic mobility of Gypsy/Travellers. It outlines the background of the struggle against discrimination in education in the UK and the EU, and demonstrates how increasingly supportive legislation has made a slow and small rise in Gypsy/Traveller numbers in schools and other educational institutions. Research from Europe and the UK is used to show the endemic issues that illustrate Traveller resistance to 'mainstream' initiatives on their behalf throughout. However, the question consistently arises whether educational efforts are viewed by them as positive or are seen to fail because Travellers are doing what they always have done and still do, and that is taking control for themselves and choosing what specific educational opportunities on offer will benefit them. Finally, the way forward is seen to lie in ensuring that Gypsy/Traveller cultures are recognised and welcomed as a critical aspect of social capital which needs to be developed, shared and acknowledged, through its transparent inclusion in the process and outcomes of education and preparation for employment.

Introduction

This paper defines the benefits or otherwise of education to support the social and economic mobility of Gypsy/Travellers. It outlines the background of the struggle against discrimination in education in the UK and the EU, and demonstrates how increasingly supportive legislation has made a slow and small rise in Gypsy/Traveller numbers in schools and other educational institutions. Research when available is used to show the endemic issues that illustrate the Traveller resistance to 'mainstream' initiatives on their behalf throughout. However, the question consistently arises whether educational efforts are viewed by them as positive or are seen to fail because Travellers are doing what they always have done and still do, and that is taking control for themselves and choosing what specific educational opportunities on offer will benefit them. They do not always want to simply accept the predicted benefits assured by the dominant culture in Europe and the UK, which are related to the educational requirements of a knowledge economy. In a knowledge economy skills are seen to be measurable in terms of the years of formal education a person receives (Becker 1964).

Education systems in Europe are built on the premise that more technological advancement will lead to a greater demand for technical, managerial and professional workers which leaves fewer jobs for those with little formal education and training (Kerr et al. 1973). Yet all economic skills are socially defined and constructed and woven into different cultural contexts, primarily through systems of education and schooling. The Gypsy/Traveller culture is traditionally a low-waged, low-skills economy which has developed from the demands of a rural economy in rural areas of Europe. Their traditional culture and way of life is under threat and education plays a large role in opening access to wider knowledge and skills, but also significantly being responsible for Travellers losing touch with their traditions and values because mainstream education does not perpetuate or understand them. The failure of education to represent their cultural needs has been repeatedly noted in research (ACE 2007; Cemlyn 2000; Decade of Roma Inclusion 2009a, 2009b; Department for Children, Schools and Families (DCSF) 2009; Department for Education and Skills 2003, 2005; Derrington and Kendall 2003, 2004, 2007; EU 2004; Jordan 2000; Kiddle 1999; Lloyd and Stead 2009; OFSTED 1996, 1999, 2001; O'Hanlon and Holmes 2004; Save the Children 2001; UNCF 2007; Warrington 2006).

The Traveller community in the EU, including the UK, comprise Romany Gypsies, Irish Travellers, Welsh Travellers, Scottish Gypsy/Travellers, New Travellers and Occupational Travellers (including show/circus/barge people). The paper will use the term Gypsy/Travellers throughout to refer to all groups, except where argument demands otherwise. Although the term Traveller suggests a homogenous group of people, there is no one single group of Travellers. Traveller and Gypsy is a collective term for all those ethnic minorities, business, professional and cultural communities who travel for work purposes or who keep travel as an option and focus in their lives when they are settled. In their own communities Travellers may assert their own specific identities within the broader Traveller terminology (Gypsy, Irish Traveller, Fairground, Circus and Show people, Bargee etc.). The 1976 Race Relations Act has identified and recognised both Gypsies and Irish Travellers in law as ethnic minority groups with a shared culture, language and beliefs (O'Hanlon and Holmes 2004). All Travellers are either seasonally or permanently mobile which leads to intermittent opportunities for their children's schooling.

Cultural identity

Many of the differences between the Gypsy/Traveller and settled communities in the EU are perpetuated by misunderstanding and labelling, because it is the established and settled institutions which organise and provide education through schooling. One label often used is that Gypsy/Travellers are 'outside of' or 'marginal' to the mainstream cultures of Europe, and consequently, they are seen to require help, economic support and educational input. The perception generally is that Gypsy/Travellers suffer social exclusion and that efforts should be made on their behalf to 'include' them, which leads to a mindset that is not helpful to these communities and may lead to misplaced policies and provision.

Gypsy/Travellers are a diverse group with a variety of cultural traditions 'with shifting boundaries of different force' (Liegeois 1994, 61). Cultural identities generally move and change and are not permanently situated in the past. Ethnic boundaries are fluid, and ascribed status can be part of an emerging self and community Traveller identity. Gypsy/Travellers have always lived on 'the margins of settled society and both mobile and sedentary cultures have been influenced reciprocally' (Mc Cluskey and Lloyd 2005, 3).

Gypsy/Travellers are perceived as living on the margins of a mainstream or dominant society, yet is important that we reflect about terms like 'marginal' used to refer to people outside the mainstream or dominant culture or existing on the fringe of society. Freire (1977) asserts that a marginal person is not 'outside of', on the contrary he is 'inside of' his/her own culture, values and lifestyle. He implies that mainstream people in any society or national context see themselves at the centre of 'something', and see the marginal person as 'sick' and in need of education or schooling. He suggests that educators or teachers often see themselves to be 'benevolent counsellors, scouring the outskirts of the city looking for stubborn illiterates', to restore them to the bosom of happiness by giving them the gift of literacy (Freire 1977, 28). This metaphor reinforces the idea that Gypsy/Traveller communities are 'sick' and in need of support and help to enable them to participate in mainstream life and take advantage of the equal opportunities offered therein. Educators assume that the cure for this condition lies in schooling/literacy to enable them to return to the 'healthy' structure or mainstream system from which they have been segregated. Marginalised people cannot overcome their dependency by simple 'inclusion' into the very structures responsible for their alienation and dependency, it needs a recognition and build up of minorities' cultural and social capital, people 'with difference' to change, contribute to, and transform mainstream society. There is always an ambiguity when institutional help is offered to minority groups, and questions are then asked about why these opportunities are rejected or ultimately seen to fail.

It is because the Gypsy/Traveller community is recognised to be a cultural minority on the margins of mainstream society that understanding how cultural reproduction operates through school systems is critical to interpreting their attitudes, and responses to the numerous high-cost educational initiatives, sponsored nationally and throughout the EU. It has been identified by Bourdieu and others (Bourdieu 1988; Bourdieu and Passeron 1977) which schools as well as other social institutions perpetuate social and economic inequalities which already exist within societies. Schools influence the learning of values, attitudes and habits, which can limit the opportunities of some, while facilitating those of others. Bernstein (1975) has demonstrated how broad cultural differences emerge through language and ways that children from minority groups talk and act, which may clash with those dominant in the school. Illich also points out that children spend long hours in school learning much more than is offered in lessons. Through the hidden curriculum children learn to 'know their place and to sit still in it' (Illich 1973). Willis reinforces this further in his classic school study where he shadows the 'lads', who saw school as an alien environment. The 'lads' realised that work could be much like school but they looked forward to it. They were impatient for wages and enjoyed the adult status which came from working, but not in making a 'lifelong' career for themselves (Willis 1981/1977). This research has parallels with Gypsy/Traveller communities where the value and foundations of mainstream schooling is often questioned. Formal schooling may be used intermittently and then rejected by them on the grounds of its inappropriateness to meet their economic needs.

Freire warns us about educating minorities for a future role in mainstream society that may not exist as time expires. Simply teaching children and adults to read and write does not work miracles, if there are not enough jobs for people in mainstream society teaching more people to read is not going to create them (Freire 1977). What

Freire is emphasising is the need to reach beyond the obvious of simply developing literacy, and try to educate people by whatever means possible to find a language to communicate what it is they want to say, and to find a means of empowerment in their 'so-called' marginalised lives. Education is then a tool for their politicisation and allows them a visibility in mainstream society. He wants them to understand what it is in the society they occupy that makes their way of life deviant or threatening to mainstream citizens. It is for them alone to decide whether to change or maintain their cultural tradition. Gypsy/Travellers want to be able to refuse education and schooling without being classified as 'criminal' or 'deviant'. In the UK today parents are sent to jail if their child/ren persistently refuse to attend school under the age of 16 years. However, there are special regulations for Gypsy/Traveller families and a large degree of tolerance for the nomadic way of life throughout the EU and particularly in the UK, as explained in the following sections. The whole notion of enforcing education, and consequently a mainstream culture, on minority peoples should be constantly questioned. When communities choose non-participation in social institutions, this should not be punished, particularly for threatened minorities who cannot survive unless they perpetuate their own traditions and cultures.

Accommodation

Traveller and Gypsy communities have had a long history of discrimination and resistance to their way of life (Kenrick and Bakewell 1995). In the UK during the post-war period as a result of increased development and changes in the law, Gypsy/Traveller families, many of whom were forced off the land they owned, found it difficult to find stopping places. This brought them into greater conflict with the settled non-Traveller community. In 1968 the Caravan Sites Act placed a duty on local authorities to establish sites for the Gypsy/Traveller community. Provision only started to grow rapidly with the allocation of 100% grants from central Government in 1980 following the recommendation of the Cripps Commission. In 1994 the Conservative government introduced the Criminal Justice and Public Order Act, which released local authorities from the duty to provide sites and has led to a reduction in provision, as some sites have closed and the Gypsy/Traveller community has grown. Gypsy/Travellers were told that a 'level playing field' would exist and they were advised to buy their own land. However, over 90% of the planning applications submitted by Gypsy/Travellers for permanent sites are refused, as opposed to 20% for the sedentary community. The cost of dealing with unauthorised sites was estimated to be £18 million per annum in 2002 (Morris and Clements 2002). It is believed that the cost is now much greater. This is seen as an unsustainable use of resources. Therefore questions are being asked about why the money is not spent to build more and better sites for Gypsy/Traveller communities (Morris & Clements 1999).

The Commission for Racial Equality in the UK has found that policies on Gypsy/Traveller sites and stopping places are not created consultatively with the people concerned. They affirm that policies on Gypsy sites (when they exist) are not informed by public consultation or information about people's actual needs for services. Most authorities do little to fill gaps in information, nor do they use the evidence of community tensions to shape their policies. The vast majority of local authorities do not collect ethnic monitoring data on the outcomes of their services for Gypsies and Irish Travellers in their area, despite the Commission for Racial Equality's advice to include sub-categories for Gypsies and Irish Travellers in their local ethnic monitoring systems. Authorities collect some information about Gypsies and Irish Travellers through the Traveller Education Service and the biannual caravan count, but this is not generally used to inform or plan their service (Commission for Racial Equality 2006).

It is now estimated that over 30% of the Traveller community live on unauthorised sites, having nowhere to stop they are sometimes forced to occupy public places (Bhopal 2000; Derrington and Kendall 2007; Jordan 2001; O'Hanlon and Holmes 2004; Power 2004; Save the Children 2001). Some of these cause great inconvenience for the housed population. Yet high-standard accommodation, with water and power, is critical for children's development and health. The poor living conditions which homeless Gypsy/Travellers endure has had a negative effect on their health and access to services. The British Medical Association has reported the Gypsy/Traveller community is the most at risk health group in the UK. They have the lowest life expectancy and the highest child mortality rates in the UK. A lack of stopping places also has a disruptive impact on Gypsy/Traveller children's education. Furthermore, OFSTED has recognised that many Gypsy/Traveller pupils suffer in society, and do not always benefit from education. Gypsy/Traveller children also experience relentless bullying at school and have low levels of educational achievement and high rates of illiteracy (OFSTED 1996). The situation is similar throughout the EU.

The UK: education

Clearly Gypsy/Travellers are included in all policy and legislation related to education in the UK. Specifically, the Education Act of 1902 extended compulsory education to the whole population and the Children's Act of 1908 specified that children of nomadic parents were required to attend for 200 half days instead of the normal 400. Yet this was rarely enforced and few children attended school. Since then numerous Education Acts 1944, 1996, 1988, have raised the school leaving age to 16 years and imposed a duty on all parents to secure the education of their children. Also, government-commissioned reports in 1967 (Plowden) and 1985 (Swann) have raised the profile of Gypsy/Traveller education, e.g. the Plowden Report described Gypsy children as 'probably the most deprived group in the country'. The Swann Report found Gypsies to be probably the most severely deprived children educationally in the country, noting that it is clear that there has been a substantial failure to meet the needs of Gypsy children (Swann Report 1985).

Government policy attempts to offer educational opportunities to all children in the UK, and Gypsy/Traveller children are subject to the same regulations as the sedentary population in terms of school attendance. When they are not travelling Gypsy/Traveller children must attend school full-time, until they reach statutory school leaving age, and Local Authorities have a duty to educate them. Yet, Gypsy/Traveller parents also have a duty to make sure their children are receiving education suitable to their needs when not in school. A significant number of Travellers know education law and their right to choose education at home. Their activities have led to groups of parents using the option of Education Otherwise (EO) (OFSTED 1996, 70: 26), which is the parents' right to choose how they fulfil their educational obligations to their children. Traveller families have always found ways to avoid schooling but are increasingly aware that EO is an option for them, although in the past they have had to educate their children themselves because of limited access to schools (Kiddle 1999). Many Traveller parents believe that they can teach their children during adolescence, especially inculcating their 'tradition and way of life', which to be preserved has to be learned and practised (Kiddle 1999).

Gypsy/Roma and Travellers of Irish Heritage are identified as racial groups and ratified by the Race Relations Act as legitimate minority ethnic communities. However, it is confirmed that Gypsy, Roma and Traveller communities experience social exclusion and discrimination (DCSF 2009). There is a pervasive and corrosive impact of experiencing racism and discrimination throughout an entire lifespan of Gypsy/Travellers in employment, social and public contexts which leads to 'cultural trauma' produced by the failings of the twenty-first-century British society and public bodies' failure to engage in an equitable manner with members of the community (Cemlyn et al. 2009, iv). Consequently, many Travellers avoid identification in official school documentation.

The DCSF states that 'the initial analysis from the ethnicity data collection since 2003 is signalling some serious concerns about the relative attainment of these groups of pupils' and 'it would seem that those pupils and parents willing to declare their specific ethnicity may be a very small percentage of the estimated cohort of these children' (2009, 12).

The report advises parents to declare their children's true identity to enable them to achieve through schooling:

> Schools and local authorities want pupils to achieve to their full potential and it is recognised that pupils who are fearful and have to deny their identity in the school setting are destined to underachieve compared with pupils who do not suffer this unfair and needless disadvantage. (DCSF 2009, 23)

The implication is that Traveller children will underachieve and be further disadvantaged in school if their ethnic origins are not declared. At the same time, however, the report recognises that pupils are fearful of schools because of issues surrounding cultural identity. Whether or not it is simply a matter of a child being seen and identified by the school as a Gypsy/Traveller and subsequently can be a school achiever is open to question. Underachievement for Traveller/Gypsy children may be much more about being immersed in a strange and different culture that is difficult for them to understand. However, there are statutory regulations which are used to enforce a minimum attendance at school. Since the 1989 Children Act, the issue of mobility and its difficulties for continuous schooling has been recognised in relation to school attendance, requiring Traveller children to attend school for a minimum of 200 school sessions (ECOTEC 2008).

The Gypsy and Traveller community in the UK is composed of Gypsies and Irish Travellers and other Traveller groups such as New Travellers. There are said to be 90,000–120,000 nomadic Gypsies and Travellers but there may be as many as a further 200,000 of Gypsy/Traveller ancestry who are living in housed accommodation. The exact figure is difficult to estimate, as their numbers are not recorded at present in census records. The school census categorisation does not include Fairground children or Occupational Travellers, children travelling with circuses, the waterways or New Travellers (DCSF 2009).

There is evidence too of a growing achievement gap that separates economically disadvantaged pupils from those who are less disadvantaged. The culture and environment in which children grow still plays a role in the achievement gap. The evidence shows that many minority children begin their educational career at a disadvantage. If children start school with small vocabularies, do not have help with homework, do not try to do well in school and are not familiar with the dominant cultural capital, these factors will influence the success or otherwise of education. Progress in closing the gap has been slow and the low achievement of minority pupils remains one of the most challenging problems in education in recent decades. Research has identified a number of factors which influence the achievement gap, e.g. pupils' cultural or racial background, their parents' educational level, access to pre-school, peer influences, teachers' expectations, and curricular and teaching quality (Hanushek and Rivkin 2006; Kosters and Mast 2003).

Education still aims to meet the needs of a literate and disciplined workforce to meet the needs of a knowledge economy. Fee-paying, 'public' schools still hold a privileged place in UK society and the formal curriculum supports cultural reproduction through organised curricula and school settings. When education does not support the minority cultures of marginalised peoples it can operate a contradictory situation, where it further excludes from mainstream society rather than includes. Many minority cultures are threatened by an inflexible mainstream education system and curricula which does not allow for cultural differences. Traveller and Gypsy children, because they live a nomadic existence and live in mobile homes, are often stereotyped and discriminated against. Their culture also affords them different values and attitudes, which settled communities and mainstream schools find difficult to understand and accept, e.g. the use of dialect, Romani or Cant.

EU policies

In a wider European context, education and schooling is developed and supported nationally for Gypsy/Traveller communities, but this is often variable and difficult to monitor. It can be accepted unquestionably that education policy in the UK, and more widely in the EU, supports and aims to develop education as far as possible as a means of equalisation through its system of universal education (O'Hanlon and Holmes 2004), yet in spite of numerous educational initiatives education tends to reaffirm existing inequalities more than it acts to change them (Bourdieu 1998; Bourdieu and Passeron 1977).

There has been a limited amount of research on Gypsy/Travellers in the UK and Europe.

European policy since 1989 towards Roma Gypsies to provide access to public services and education has changed since the collapse of communism and the process of European re-integration. Over three-quarters of the Roma Gypsies live in the former communist countries of Central and South-Eastern Europe which leads to considerable differences in their demographic distribution, and their historical, social, economic and cultural situation. However, there are often as many divisions within countries as there are between them. Central and South-Eastern Europe has much larger urban populations of Roma Gypsies than Western Europe where they have been exposed more to majority cultural norms than their Western Europe neighbours (Save the Children 2001, 11).

A study of the education of Occupational Travellers in the EU has recently been published (ECOTEC 2008) which presents an overview of the education policies of member states. The study takes it as given that education is both a universal right for citizens and is therefore compulsory by law, but this also confers certain responsibilities on all EU states to:

- Ensure attendance at school.
- Allocate responsibility for follow-up and avoidance of absence.
- Ensure that schooling is accessible and relevant by providing enough school places, appropriate teaching and opportunities for accreditation.

Although aims are high for the Lisbon objectives in education and training there are still concerns about the increasing number of early school leavers among Gypsy/Traveller communities and their failure to complete upper secondary education. The Race Relations (Amendment) Act (2000) in the UK places a duty on schools to monitor the impact of their provision on the achievement of their pupils, including on those from Gypsy/Traveller backgrounds. Moreover, when undergoing an inspection, schools need to be able to show that they are supporting the education of absent pupils, such as offering good quality distance learning opportunities and keeping in close contact with Gypsy/Traveller children via a range of strategies including information and communication technologies. In the UK and throughout the EU it has been observed that some Gypsy/Travellers do not value traditional methods of education, due to their tendency to involve children in the family business from an early age. Also, the family plays a key educational role in Gypsy/Traveller communities, but little attention has been paid to its values and dynamics in educational contexts. Many factors constrain educational achievement for Gypsy/Traveller children, namely interrupted learning and the associated problems such as lack of continuity, repetition, lack of assessment, and difficulties in forming relationships with teachers and fellow pupils. Language difficulties may also constrain learning because children travelling to different countries with their parents face additional obstacles in the form of language barriers (EUMC 2006).

Evidence of the inequalities and disadvantages faced by many Gypsy/Travellers generally is unambiguous. For example, in Ireland recent research has shown that they endure some of the worst living conditions, with high levels of overcrowding or unsuitable accommodation, which lacks basic amenities. Poor living conditions and high levels of disease all contribute to ill health. Overall, the life expectancy of Gypsy/Travellers is 20 years less than that of the settled community while infant mortality rates are three times higher than the general population. Socio-economic factors, such as long-term unemployment, educational difficulties and poor living conditions have contributed to Gypsy/Travellers experiencing significantly lower levels of health than the majority settled community. Attitudes towards Gypsy/Travellers are significantly more negative than towards any other ethnic minority group (DENI 2006).

Similarly, in Cambridgeshire, recent research reports that Gypsy/Travellers are the minority most overlooked by service providers and policy makers. They have low health status, a higher likelihood of homelessness and are most at risk at school. The experience of racism left Gypsy/Traveller children with a sense of vulnerability and exposure to risk with additional anxieties related to finding safe and authorised sites and stopping places to prevent being constantly moved on (Warrington 2006).

In the wider EU situation the same picture emerges with the Roma/Gypsies' and Travellers' long history of, and the continued pervasiveness, of anti-Roma/Gypsy and Traveller prejudice, racism and related intolerance (Save the Children 2001, 13).

George Soros, in his keynote address to the first ever EU Roma summit to celebrate the Decade of Roma Inclusion in 2008, states that Roma discrimination is the worst in the EU:

To say that the Roma do not enjoy equal opportunity is an understatement. I can testify from personal knowledge that many Roma families and communities live in sub-human conditions. An unacceptable reality gives rise to a negative stereotype and the negative stereotype makes the situation of the Roma worse. The net result is the worst case of discrimination and social exclusion based on ethnicity in the European Union. (Soros 2008)

He proceeds with the observation that funds and incentives used by national governments in Europe are not popular with the electorates of the countries concerned because of the negative stereotype that prevails, yet the affirmative programmes are designed to apply to socially excluded people (like Travellers) in general, and not just the Roma.

However, despite lack of data for specific ethnic groups like Roma, Gypsy and Traveller, the literature suggests that achievement amongst these EU Traveller communities is generally low across all member states. Many Roma are educated in special or ghetto schools where standards of teaching and facilities are poor. Existing evidence shows that Roma are significantly under-represented at secondary level and in higher education with poor attendance and underachievement (Ringold et al. 2005). Roma lack pre-school education, which is crucial for early assimilation of school norms, expected behaviour patterns, and language acquisition (UNICEF 2007, cited in DCSF 2009). More significantly, institutional factors have been identified which discriminate against Roma communities including the absence of Traveller-related curriculum resources and a lack of training for teachers to enable them to teach ethnically mixed classes (EUMC 2006). The Report notes that there are significant similarities between the situation of Gypsy/Traveller communities in the UK and that of Roma across Europe. The UK would appear to have better developed inter-cultural practice but there is evidence that there is still a long way to go before the curricula (generally in the EU) fully affirms the identity, history and culture of all Gypsy/Traveller pupils, and they can feel safe from racist bullying and abuse' (DCSF 2009, 11).

Throughout the UK, Ireland and the rest of the EU the majority of the Gypsy/Traveller pupils experience 'interrupted learning'. Many Gypsy/Travellers do not attend school out of fear of racist attacks and because of what they see as a continuing lack of relevance of the secondary curriculum. It is particularly irrelevant for boys, who continue to attend primary school precisely to catch up on basic literacy and numeracy skills. An Irish research study of Gypsy/Traveller teachers' evidence demonstrated that flexible arrangements in schools and out-of-school settings could not deliver sufficient educational input comparable with their mainstream peers, reflecting a picture of impoverished and missed educational opportunity (DENI 2006).

By way of a European-wide solution ECOTEC (2008) recommends that because of the distribution and movement of Traveller communities, particularly occupational Travellers, there should be a move towards tailored learning pathways, which focus on 'learning outcomes' rather than attendance at school, as the most suitable approach to educating Traveller children. It is a shift away from the idea of equality of opportunities to equality of outcomes and reflects similar developments across education and training policy in Europe (ECOTEC 2008, 7). More significantly, the Green Paper entitled 'Migration and Mobility: Challenges and Opportunities for EU Education Systems', takes the view that policies significantly influence school performance, and notes that those systems that strongly prioritise equity in education are also the most effective in integrating migrant pupils (Europa Brussels 2008). The Green Paper recommends the use of inclusive education, rather than segregated schooling, and how to adapt teaching skills to form closer links with migrant families and communities. To improve equity it advises on how to accommodate the diversity of mother tongues and cultural perspectives to build intercultural skills in the EU (Europa Brussels 2008). This further reinforces the view that Traveller communities need acceptance and recognition of their cultural traditions, especially their different languages and literacies, particularly a recognition of differences in communication not primarily dependent on national or mainstream written conventions.

Secondary schooling

Secondary-level schooling is the predominant issue for all Gypsy/Traveller communities. Gypsy/Traveller children are seen to reach maturity and adulthood early in their teens and are expected to 'work' and follow the traditional patterns of their families. As a consequence, secondary school curricula aimed to satisfy a mainstream knowledge economy is not relevant for these needs. Gypsy/Traveller children are at extreme risk of failing to transfer to secondary school and many choose to absent themselves. OFSTED comments:

> Access to the curriculum for secondary aged children remains a matter of grave concern. There are possibly as many as 10,000 children at this phase who are not even registered with a school. (1996, 14)

A recent government initiative in the area of Information and Communication Technology (ICT) and multimedia resources for pupils is also being reviewed for its impact on Traveller education. Furthermore, the 'Sure Start' programmes introduced initially in England, Wales and Scotland and then later Northern Ireland, aim at improving the health and education status of 0–3-year-olds by activities targeted at children and families. For older pupils, the government introduced a £420 million youth support service called 'Connexions' in 2001. The aim of this service was to offer the best start in life for every young person and to offer a range of guidance and support for 13–19-year-olds, to help make the transition to adult life a smooth one (OFSTED 1999).

In 2003 'Aiming High', a government strategy to raise the achievement of ethnic minority pupils, offered another opportunity to make sure that concerns about educational attainment among Gypsy/Traveller pupils formed a distinct strand within the strategy. In this context the Ministry of Education published a specific guide for schools (Department for Education and Skills 2003).

In Scotland, there was no special grant for Gypsy/Traveller education as in England and Wales and funding was allocated within the overall framework of funding for local authorities. The 2001 'Inquiry into Travellers and Public Sector Policies' demonstrated the need for positive change at local authority and individual school level and the Scottish Executive introduced in 2003 guidance for all education authorities and schools. As is recognised generally in the UK, attendance and attainment of Gypsy/Travellers in schools and in out-of-school settings show that 'the aim of the National Priorities to deliver the best possible life chance for every child' is a long way from being realised for many Gypsy/Traveller pupils (Padfield and Jordan 2004).

However, raising the school leaving age has caused tensions between Traveller families and school authorities. Many young people choose not to attend secondary schooling even when it is provided for them. Parents may choose the 'Education Otherwise' option instead of formal schooling, to teach and prolong their traditional way of life:

> In the UK the raising of the school leaving age to 16 and subsequent developments in education policy towards an increasingly academic curriculum over the past twenty years has effectively defined and consolidated this particular cultural boundary. (DCSF 2009,6)

Evidence throughout the EU suggests that Gypsy/Traveller parents' expectations are that sons and daughters should follow traditional and cultural gender-based roles in adult life, with the assumption that their children leave school at 14 years. However, the education of Gypsy/Travellers in the EU has been most effective where a wider national policy framework has supported innovative local provision. In countries where provision is devolved to regional level, variation in the level and quality of provision has been found (ECOTEC 2008).

Employment and social inclusion

Within the EU, since the Lisbon Treaty, the strategy for jobs, growth and social cohesion has led to the redesign of provision and education and training to develop a human capital more suitable to the requirements of the new vision of the knowledge-based society in Europe. Although the Education Council in May 2007 adopted 16 core indicators for monitoring progress towards the Lisbon objectives, progress overall has been less than planned. The children of occupational Travellers still have problems with access, rights of access, discontinuity, discrimination and provision of open, flexible and distance learning. Evidence indicates that these children perform poorly against some of the Lisbon core indicators, namely early school leaving and the completion of upper secondary education (ECOTEC 2008).

Education and Training within the EU has been reviewed since the inception of the Lisbon Strategy for jobs, growth and social cohesion in order to develop social capital to meet the requirements of the new knowledge economy (ibid.). A new initiative has been launched for social cohesion in the twenty-first century. However, national education policies vary across the 27 member states because of the size, nature, diversity and visibility of Gypsy/Traveller communities, which leads to a variation in their level of need.

Research has shown that the issues of accommodation and racism have shaped Gypsy/Travellers' access to employment and social activities, as well as to education (DCSF 2009; Decade of Roma Inclusion 2009a, 2009b). A second factor that has shaped Gypsy/Travellers' general social inclusion is the age structure of the population. Because the age profile for the Gypsy/Traveller population is in marked contrast to that for the national population, a very high proportion of Gypsy/Travellers are in the childhood and youth age bands (likely to be in education) and a very low proportion is over 65 years old.

Travellers are self-employed by tradition. Historically their economic activities served the local farm population and included casual migrant labouring, trade in farm animals, and making and mending tin ware. Market trading and scrap collecting are currently two major areas of activity in the UK and Ireland. Also, growing numbers are finding employment in the building and service sectors. However, there is evidence that parents are encouraging their children to accept school-based education to develop the skills necessary to adapt to changing employment patterns (Cemlyn and Clark 2005).

Differences in economic development affect the opportunities for European Roma Gypsies too and there are similarities between the situation of the Roma in the UK with that of Roma across Europe (Wilkin, Derrington, and Foster 2009). In the former communist states of Europe Roma/Gypsies were usually targeted for low-skilled employment within a centrally planned economy, in both industry and agriculture. Since the transition to the EU, widespread unemployment and a dependence on restricted state benefits and services have led to economic difficulties for Roma/Gypsies, exacerbating the gap between the more- or less-developed countries particularly between Northern and South, East and Central Europe (Save the Children 2001).

Research in the EU generally is hampered by a paucity of relevant official data and the different data collection methodologies employed makes data comparability practically impossible. In most countries transition to secondary education is reportedly particularly low, and even in countries where more Gypsy/Traveller pupils seem to continue their studies in secondary education to some extent (such as in Austria, the Netherlands, Hungary, England and Wales), they regularly choose vocational rather than general secondary education, while drop-out rates are very high. Participation in higher education is practically non-existent in all countries. In some countries, notably Belgium and France, enrolment and attendance varies between different groups (EUMC 2006).

Absenteeism in schools remains a persistent, common and serious problem that needs to be addressed effectively by understanding the underlying causes. Access to education and the educational attainment of Gypsy/Travellers is affected by direct and systemic discrimination in, and exclusion from, education and influenced by their overall conditions of life, which are invariably characterised by high unemployment, substandard housing and poor access to health services, creating a vicious circle of poverty, exclusion and marginalisation that affects their ability to participate in and benefit from education (EUMC 2006).

The importance attached by the family and the community to education has also a profound impact on the children's willingness to attend school regularly and learn effectively. Evidence suggests that Gypsy/Traveller communities are aware of the benefits of formal education, but its actual capacity to improve their future life chances depends also upon prevailing prejudice and discrimination in the labour market. The school itself also influences how Gypsy/Traveller pupils experience education through the way it interacts with them, their families and their community (DCSF 2009).

Collaboration between professionals and organisations working with Gypsy/Travellers and other mobile families, like the Traveller Education Support Service, has proved effective in protecting children's rights to education.

However, poor understanding of the culture and values of Gypsy/Traveller groups can mean that traditional educational provision appears of little relevance to them. There is a mismatch between pupils' learning needs and traditional educational provision throughout the EU generally, and transition from primary to secondary-level education appears to be a particular issue. It is important for school provision to be flexible in order to recognise the skills Gypsy/Traveller children develop informally, in the home or in the family business, and to build on these skills in order to provide relevant and accessible curricula, in or out of school. Accessible curricula may be defined by the content and process of education, particularly schooling.

Recent EU research has shown that success with Roma communities' schooling increased when there was a greater emphasis on the integration of cultural education activities in the classroom or the pursuit of other activities which advance intercultural education, especially instructional materials on Roma history, culture and traditions. It also reported that most success was achieved through a culture of supported risk taking and experimentation with the curriculum, a positive attitude to Roma/Gypsy students and high expectations for them to succeed (Decade of Roma Inclusion 2009b).

In the UK specifically the DCSF (2009) report advises the need for greater flexibility of, and recognition of, Gypsy/Traveller culture within the curriculum because pupils and teachers from the settled community may have negative perceptions and prejudices regarding pupils from Gypsy/Traveller communities, which interfere with their assimilation in schools. This was recognised in the Roma research as a barrier to progress rectified by more specific targeted Gypsy/Traveller content in teacher training and education. The report recommends increased and more appropriate formal training, and opportunities for both new and practising teachers, which are quality assured. Training programmes also need to be incorporated into wider policy objectives and designed with Gypsy/Traveller input to ensure their cultural appropriateness. These and many other factors raise a number of common concerns about future successful educational provision throughout the EU.

Conclusion

It has been shown thatGypsy/Traveller communities in recent years have similar issues and problems throughout the EU countries including the UK and Ireland.

Enrolment and attendance rates of Gypsy/Traveller pupils are generally poor especially in comparison with those of the general population. Gypsy/Traveller pupils tend to leave education early without the qualifications that would enable them to compete successfully in the labour market.

When the above are integrated with the absence of systematic monitoring of key indicators, such as enrolment, attendance, attainment and performance of Gypsy/Traveller pupils, jobs and work, as well as institutional structural discrimination and racist incidents, it makes for a generally problematic systemic situation in education and employment to be overcome.

Traveller and Gypsy communities in the EU and the UK are in some sense resentful of the pressures placed on them to send their children to school, particularly secondary education. They are empowered in another sense to have the choice of being allowed to decide for themselves what is appropriate for their own needs. It appears that there are some who do not want change or have any interference in their way of life, but these traditional Gypsy/Traveller attitudes may be dying out. New generations of Gypsy/Travellers are more inclined to take advantage of educational opportunities, as and when appropriate, to meet their needs. Yet overall, they do not like the compulsory nature of schooling that interferes with their migrant lifestyle and imposes 'rules' regarding school attendance on specific dates at specific times, and travel and dress for attendance at school institutions. Education, and more exactly, schooling systems within Western economic systems, based on capitalism, with banks, imposed taxes, compulsory insurance etc. are not supportive of their traditional migrant lifestyle.

Gypsy/Travellers' community work skills are acquired by interacting with other family and community members and can be more important than formal education provided by the school. The acquisition of traditional work skills is vital, particularly for those who move frequently, due to the important contribution children make to their family's economic activities. These skills are not only technical, but also more importantly social, based on co-operation and networks, including teamwork, and the flexibility to adapt to change and develop intercultural competencies. However, since access to the labour market in the knowledge society largely depends on academic qualifications, low levels of schooling are a serious barrier to school leavers when acquiring employment. However, there needs to be an acknowledgement and respect for the value of education provided within Gypsy/Traveller communities and families, and it is important to involve parents in extending their cultural work by respecting and building upon their values, structures, languages and lifestyle. The way forward lies in ensuring that Gypsy/Traveller cultures are recognised and welcomed as a critical aspect of social capital which needs to be developed, shared and acknowledged, through its transparent inclusion in the process and outcomes of education and preparation for employment. This can be achieved by valuing Gypsy/Traveller culture and identity through the political development of community cohesion and action programmes that are democratic and transparent with guaranteed shared economic outcomes.

References

Advisory Centre for Education (ACE). 2007. *Supporting children with mobile lifestyles.* London: Ask ACE. 1,1, 18–19.
Becker, G. 1964. *Human capital: A theoretical and empirical analysis with special reference to education.* Princeton, NJ: Princeton University Press.
Bernstein, B. 1975. *Class, codes and control.* Vol. 3, *Towards a theory of educational transmission.* London: Routledge and Kegan Paul.
Bhopal, K., J. Gundara, C. Jones, and C. Owen. 2000. *Working towards inclusive education for gypsy/traveller pupils.* London: DFEE.
Bourdieu, P. 1988. *Language and symbolic power.* Cambridge: Polity Press.
Bourdieu, P., and J.-C. Passeron. 1977. *Reproduction: In education, society and culture.* London: Sage.
Cemlyn, S. 2000. *Policy and provision by social services for traveller children and families: Report on research study,* 141–52. Bristol: University of Bristol Press.
Cemlyn, S., and C. Clark. 2005. The social exclusion of Gypsy and Traveller children. In *At greatest risk: The children most likely to be poor,* ed. G. Preston, 141–52. London: Child Poverty Action Group.
Cemlyn, S., M. Greenfields, S. Burnett, Z. Matthews, and C. Whitwell. 2009. *Inequalities experienced by Gypsy and Traveller communities: A review.* London: Equality and Human Rights Commission.
Commission for Racial Equality (CRE). 2006. *Common good: Equality, good race relations and sites for Gypsies and Irish Travellers: Report of CRE inquiry in England and Wales.* London: Commission for Racial Equality (CRE).
Decade of Roma Inclusion. 2009a. Decade of Roma Inclusion 2005–2015. Decade action plans. http://www.romadecade.org/index/ (accessed July 27, 2009).
Decade of Roma Inclusion. 2009b. *Final report 157.* http://www.romadecade.org/portal/downloads/Education%20resources (accessed July 27, 2009).
Department for Children, Schools and Families. 2009. *The inclusion of Gypsy, Roma and Traveller children and young people.* London: Department for Children, Schools and Families.
Department of Education, Northern Ireland (DENI). 2006. *A response to the PSI working group report on Travellers.* Belfast: Department of Education.

Department for Education and Skills. 2000. *Race Relations Amendment Act 2000.* London: HMSO.
Department for Education and Skills. 2003. *Aiming high: Raising the achievement of Gypsy and Traveller pupils – A guide to good practice.* http://www.standards.dfes.gov.uk/ethnicminorities/links_and_publications/763027/Gypsy_Travel (accessed November 10, 2009).
Derrington, C., and S. Kendall. 2003. The experiences and perceptions of Gypsy Traveller pupils in English secondary schools. In *Encouraging voices,* ed. M. Shelvin and R. Rose. Dublin: National Disability Authority.
Derrington, C., and S. Kendall. 2004. *Gypsy Traveller students in secondary schools: Culture, identity and achievement.* Stoke on Trent, UK: Trentham Books.
Derrington, C., and S. Kendall. 2007. Challenges and barriers to secondary education: The experiences of young Gypsy Traveller students in English secondary schools. *Social Policy and Society* 7, no. 1: 1–10.
Education and Culture of the European Commission (ECOTEC). 2008. *Study on the school education of children of Occupational Travellers in the EU.* Birmingham, UK: ECOTEC.
European Union (EU). 2004. *The situation of the Roma in an enlarged European Union.* European Commission, Luxembourg. Office for Official Publications of the European Communities.
European Monitering Centre on Racism and Xenophobia (EUMC). 2006. *Roma and Travellers in public education: An overview of the situation in the EU member states: Executive summary.* Brussels: EUMC.
Europa Brussels. 2008. *Renewed social agenda: The elements of the package.* Memo/08/471, July.
Freire, P. 1977. *Cultural action for freedom.* London: Penguin Books.
Hanushek, E., and S. Rivkin. 2006. *School quality and the Black–White achievement gap.* Washington, DC: Brookings Institution Press.
Illich, I. 1973. *Deschooling society.* London: Penguin Books.
Jordan, E. 2000. Outside the mainstream. In *Edinburgh, Scottish School Board Association Millenium Book.* ed. A. Hill.
Jordan, E. 2001. Exclusion of travellers in state schools. *Educational Research* 43, no. 2: 117–32.
Kendrick, D., and S. Bakewell. 1995. *On the verge: The gypsies of England.* Hertfordshire: University of Hertfordshire Press.
Kerr, C., J. Dunlop, F. Harbison, and C. Meyer. 1973. *Industrialism and industrial man.* Harmondsworth, UK: Penguin.
Kiddle, C. 1999. *Traveller children.* London: Jessica Kingsley Publishers.
Kosters, M., and B. Mast. 2003. *Closing the achievement gap.* Washington, D.C.: AEI American Enterprise Institute, Public Policy Research.
Liegeois, J.P. 1994. *Romas, gypsies and travellers.* Strasbourg: Council of Europe.
Lloyd, G., and J. Stead. 2002. Including gypsy travellers in education. *Race Equality Teaching* 21, no. 1: 21–4.
McCluskey, G., and G. Lloyd. 2005. Schooling and Gypsy/Travellers – a complex and challenging relationship. Unpublished paper.
Morris, R., and L. Clements. 1999. *Gaining ground: Law reform and gypsies and travellers.* Hertfordshire: University of Hertfordshire Press.
Morris, R., and L. Clements. 2002. The economics of Gypsy and Traveller encampments. http://www.travellerslaw.org.uk/issues.htm (accessed November 21, 2008).
O'Hanlon, C., and P. Holmes. 2004. *The education of Gypsy and Traveller children.* Stoke on Trent, UK: Trentham Books.
Office for Standards in Education (OFSTED). 1996. *The education of travelling children.* London: OFSTED.
Office for Standards in Education (OFSTED). 1999. *Raising the attainment of minority ethnic pupils.* London: OFSTED.
Office for Standards in Education (OFSTED). 2001. *Managing support for the attainment of pupils from minority ethnic groups.* London: OFSTED.
Padfield, P., and E. Jordan. 2004. *Issues in school enrolment, attendance, attainment and support for learning for Gypsy/Travellers and school-aged children and young people*

based in Scottish Local Authority sites. Edinburgh: Moray House School of Education, Scottish Traveller Education Programme.

Plowden Report. 1967. *Children and their primary schools: A report of the Central Advisory Council for Education.* London: Her Majesty's Stationery Office.

Power, C. 2004. *Room to roam: England's Irish travellers.* London, Irish Traveller Movement in Britain, http://www.irishtraveller.org.uk/wp-content/uploads/2007/2008/room_to_roam.pdf (accessed July 23, 2009).

Ringold, D., Orenstein, M.A., and E. Wilkens. 2005. *Roma in an expanding Europe: Breaking the poverty cycle.* Washington DC: The World Bank.

Save the Children. 2001. *Denied a future? The right to education of Roma/Gypsy and Traveller children.* London: Save the Children.

Soros, G. 2008. An unacceptable reality: The situation of Roma in the European Union. Keynote address to the EU Roma Summit, September 16, in Brussels Open Society Institute and Soros Foundation Network.

Swann Report. 1985. *Education for all: Report of the Committee of Enquiry into the education of children from ethnic minority groups* (Chairman: Lord Swann). London: Her Majesty's Stationery Office.

United Nations Children's Fund (UNCF). 2007. *Breaking the cycle of exclusion: Roma children in South East Europe.* Paris: UNICEF organisation.

Warrington, C. 2006. Gypsy and Traveller children ought to be engaged more by mainstream services. Communitycare.co.uk/articles (accessed July 27, 2009).

Wilkin, A., C. Derrington, and B. Foster. 2009. *Improving the outcomes for Gypsy, Roma and Traveller pupils.* Slough, Berkshire: NFER.

Willis, P. 1981/1977. *Learning to labour. How working class kids get working class jobs.* New York: Columbia University Press.

Index

Page numbers in *Italics* represent tables.

Abrar, C.: and Siddiqui, T. 4
Advisory Centre for Education (ACE) 104
Aiming High 112
amader (our) culture 24–7
Amin, S. 13–16; and Huq, L. 12–15; and Mahmud, S. 12–15; Newby, M. and Naved, R. 16; Selim, N. and Kamal Waiz, N. 12–16
Anderson, B. 50–2
Andorka, R. 70
Annual Status of Education Review (ASER) 42
Appadurai, A. 33
Arnett, J. 95–6
Arnot, M.: and Fennell, S. 3
Atlantic Canadian rural community 6, 87–101; cosmopolitanism and education decision-making 87–99; local attachment intensity 91–4; schooling and graduation 87–99; youth aspirations and brain drain 6, 87–99
attiyo swajan (relatives and neighbours) 13, 22
autonomy 12

Baeck, D. 89
Bakewell, S.: and Kendrick, D. 106
Balagopalan, S. 33
balwadi (day-care centre) 38, 45
Bandgladesh Rural Advancement Committee (BRAC) 12
Bandyopadhyay, M.: and Govinda, R. 32
Bangladesh 5, 11–29; class, marriage and compliance 15–19, 22–7; demographic and policy-oriented research 12–13; employment and independence 19–23; fieldwork schools and colleges 14–27; higher education for girls 5, 11–27; literacy rate 13; parent choices, culture and tradition 12–27; self-hood and testimonies 15–26; staying on at school 15–19

Bangladesh Bureau of Educational Information and Statistics (BANBEIS) 13, 17–18
Bangladesh Demographic and Health Surveys 18
bari (extended family) 13
barolok (rich) 16–17
Basu, A.: and Jeffrey, R. 12
Baulch, B.: and Davis, P. 79–81
Bauman, Z. 96–7
Beck, U. 96–7
Becker, G. 103
Begum Rokeya College 14–27
Benei, V. 5–6, 63–76
Bernstein, B. 105
Berry, W. 87
Bertaux, D.: and Bertaux-Wiame, I. 64–6, 70; and Thompson, P. 2, 4, 63–6, 70
Bertaux-Wiame, I.: and Bertaux, D. 64–6, 70
Béteille, A. 64–5
Bhopal, K. 107
bikka garib (extremely poor) 16–18
Bjarnason, T.: and Thorlindsson, T. 89
Blanden, J.: Gregg, P. and Machin, S. 2
Boddy, J. 71
bondhi (tied) 22
Bourdieu, P. 31, 34, 67–8, 73, 87–8, 99, 105; and Passeron, J. 3, 32–4, 41–2, 105, 109
Bowers, C. 90
Bowles, S.: *et al* 33–4; Gintis, H. and Groves, M. 4
boyoshko (marriageable age) 16
Breman, J. 33
Bremen, J. 79
British Medical Association (BMA) 107
Brown, A.: and Kirpal, S. 52
burqa and use of veiling 25

Caddell, M. 31; and Day Ashley, L. 3
Caldwell, B. 12–13
Caravan Sites Act 106
Care Standards Act (2000) 52
Carnoy, M. 60

INDEX

Carr, P.: and Kefalas, M. 88–91
Cemlyn, S. 104; and Clark, C. 114; *et al* 108
certification effect 42–3
Chadnagar 14–27
Children, Schools and Families, Department for (DCSF) 104, 108, 111–15
Children's Act (1908) 107
Chopra, R. 24
chronic poverty 6, 77–86; inter-generational transfer 79; marginal returns 78–80; research and testimonies 81–4; and schooling 6, 77–85
Chronic Poverty Research Centre 78
Clark, C.: and Cemlyn, S. 114
Cleland, J.: *et al* 12
Clements, L.: and Morris, R. 106
cluster resource centre (CRC) 37
Collins, J. 3, 33
Commission for Racial Equality 106–7
Commonwealth Secretariat 4; Teacher Recruitment Protocol 4
Communist Party of India (CPI) 69
Connexions 112
Corbett 5–6, 77, 87–101
Corbin, J.: and Strauss, A. 55
cosmopolitanism and educational decision-making 87–101; Atlantic Canadian rural community 87–99; curriculum relevance 91–2; local attachment intensity 91–4; non-academic identities 88–99; parallel graduation celebrations 91–4; secondary schooling 88–94; testimonials 88, 91–8; timing and pressure 94–6; youth aspirations and brain drain 87–99
Cote, J. 96
Crapanzano, V. 70
Criminal Justice and Public Order Act 106
Cripps Commission 106
Crowne, F. 49
Cuban, S. 5–6, 49–62
Curran, S. 2
CV-building experiences 97–9

Dahiwale, S. 65–6
Davies, A.: and Haour-Knipe, M. 50–2, 56
Davis, P.: and Baulch, B. 79–81
Day Ashley, L.: and Caddell, M. 3
De Neve, G. 12
Decade of Roma Inclusion 104, 110, 113–15
Del Franco, N. 5–6, 11–29
Dercon, S. 80, 84
Derrington, C.: Foster, B. and Wilkin, A. 114; and Kendall, S. 104, 107
determinism 5–6, 63–76; mobility and the untouchable family 5–6
Development Research Centre (DRC) 3
disembedding of citizens 90–1

Dreze, J.: and Sen, A. 3
Dufflo, E. 79
Dumont, L. 65
Durkheim, E. 90
Dyer, C.: and Rose, P. 3, 78

Economist Intelligence Unit 13
Education Acts 107
Education Council 113
Education and Culture of the European Commission (ECOTEC) 108–13; Migration and Mobility Green Paper 111–12
Education Department, Northern Ireland (DENI) 110–11
Education For All programme 3, 37
Education Otherwise (EO) 107, 113
Education and Skills Department 104, 112
Edwards, A.: and Ureta, M. 1
Ehrenreich, B.: and Hochschild, A. 50
Elliott, B. 70–3
English for Speakers of Other Languages (ESOL) 55, 61
Erikson, E. 97
Erikson, R.: and Goldthorp, J. 2, 33
ethnic minority groups and formal education (India) 5, 31–47; gendered educational choices 31–46
European Monitoring Centre on Racism and Xenophobia (EUMC) 110–14
Ewing, K. 11
export processing zones (EPZ) 16

family and local contexts 4; Bangladesh 11–27
Fennell, S.: and Arnot, M. 3
Foster, B.: Wilkin, A. and Derrington, C. 114
Freire, P. 105–6

Gardener, K.: and Osella, F. 1
garib (poor) 16–17
Gaudet, S. 96
gender equality 12; and differences 35
gendered educational choices 31–47; access and distinctions 37; government schools and segregation 37–41; inter-generational mobility strategy 32–5; Jharkhand village 31–46; literacy levels by ethnicity *36*; private 36, 39–44; as a process 44–5; village ethnicity and contexts 34–7; white-collar employment prospects 45
George, S. 52
Ghatge Patil Industries (G.P.I.) 66
Giddens, A. 90, 96–7
Gintis, H.: Groves, M. and Bowles, S. 4
Giroux, H. 34
Glewwe, P. 79

INDEX

global care industry 50–1
globalisation 3–4
Gold, A.: and Raheja, G. 11
Goldthorp, J.: and Erikson, R. 2, 33
Gordon, S. 50
Government of India 35–6
Govinda, R.: and Bandyopadhyay, M. 32
Gramsci, A. 14, 25–7
Green, B.: and Letts, W. 87, 90
Green, M.: and Hulme, D. 80
Gregg, P.: Machin, S. and Blanden, J. 2
Groves, M.: Bowles, S. and Gintis, H. 4
Gupta, D. 64
Gypsy/Traveller communities 6, 103–18; accommodation 106–7; culture and tradition 104–8; education 107–9, 112–13; employment and social inclusion 113–15; enrolment and attendance rates 113–15; EU policies 109–12

Hanushek, E.: and Rivkin, S. 109
Haour-Knipe, M.: and Davies, A. 50–2, 56
Harriss-White, B. 79
Hashim, I. 2
Hattam, R.: and Smyth, J. 88
Haynes, D.: and Prakash, G. 11
higher education for girls (Bangladesh) 5, 11–29
Higher Secondary Certificate (HSC) 15–17
Hindus: gendered educational choices 31–46; Jharkhand (East India) 31–46; teachers 38–40
Hochschild, A.: and Ehrenreich, B. 50
Holdsworth, C. 88
Holmes, P.: and O'Hanlon, C. 107–9
Hossain, N. 12
Hulme, D.: and Green, M. 80; and Sen, B. 78
Huq, L.: and Amin, S. 12–15

Illich, I. 105
India 5, 31–47; ethnic, gender and social identity 34–46; gendered educational choices 5, 31–46; Hindus, Muslims and Scheduled Tribes (STs) 32–46; untouchable communities 63–76
Industrial and Training Institute (ITI) 66
International English Language Test System (IELTS) 53, 57, 61
International Labour Organisation (ILO) 52, 61
involved parenting 94–6
Islam, M.: Seeley, J. and Maddox, B. 78, 83

Jackson, C.: and Rao, N. 33
Jamieson, L. 89
Jarvis, P. 52

Jeffrey, P.: and Jeffrey, R. 11–12, 24–6; Jeffrey, R. and Jeffrey, C. 1–3, 77
Jeffrey, R.: and Basu, A. 12
Jharkhand (East India) 31–47; Education Department 37; gendered educational choices 31–47; Mahari Middle School 38–40, *38*; Mission schools 39–45; social hierarchies and power relations 34–46; Village Education Committee (VEC) 38
jogajog (social connections) 21
Jones, G. 89
Jordan, E. 104, 107; and Padfield, P. 112

Kabeer, N. 11
Kakar, S. 11
Kamal Waiz, N.: Amin, S. and Selim, N. 12–16
Kandiyoti, D. 26
Kaviraj, S. 65
Kefalas, M.: and Carr, P. 88–91
Kelly, P.: and Kenway, J. 51
Kelly, U. 91
Kendall, S.: and Derrington, C. 104, 107
Kendrick, D.: and Bakewell, S. 106
Kenway, J.: and Kelly, P. 51
Kerr, C.: *et al* 104
Khan, I.: and Seeley, J. 78, 84
Kiddle, C. 104, 107–8
Kingma, M. 49–55
Kirpal, S.: and Brown, A. 52
Kofman, E.: and Raghuram, P. 51, 60
Kolhapur New High School 69–70
Kosters, M.: and Mast, B. 109
Kothari Commission Report 66
Kothari, U. 3
Kumar, K. 33

Lahire, B. 65
Lalmatiya coal mines 35
Lareau, A. 94–5
Learning Skills Council 51
Leclerc-Olive, M. 68, 71
Lefebvre, H. 90
Lehmann, W. 88
Letts, W.: and Green, B. 87, 90
Liegeois, J. 104
Lisbon Treaty 110, 113
Lloyd, G.: and McCluskey, G. 105; and Stead, J. 104
lok kharap bolbe (people will say bad things) 22
Longwe, S. 12, 32
Lynch, K. 34

McCluskey, G.: and Lloyd, G. 105
Machin, S.: Blanden, J. and Gregg, P. 2
McKenzie, D.: and Rapoport, H. 4

INDEX

McLeod, A. 11, 26
McNeil-Walsh, C. 51
Maddox, B. 5–6, 77–86; Islam, M. and Seeley, J. 78, 83
madrasas (Quranic schools) 20, 36, 41–5
Maharashtra (Untouchable communities) 63–74
Mahars, Mangs and Chambhars 65–8
Mahatma Jyotirao Phule 66
Mahmud, S.: and Amin, S. 12–15
majhari (middle level earners) 16–18
matobars (village elders) 22
Mehrotra, S.: and Panchamukhi, P. 42
mene nite hobe (must be accepted) 22
methodological imperatives 4–5
Mexican migrants 4
Millennium Development Goal 12
Miller, D. 34
Mills and Boon (romantic fiction) 49–50, 61
Mission schools (East India) 39–45; Holy Cross 41–2; St James (Pathra) 39–44
mobility: pathways 2–4
Mohanty, C. 26
Mohlis/bamboo workers 35
Molgat, M. 96
Momsen, J. 52
Morgan, J.: *et al* 4
Morris, R.: and Clements, L. 106
Mosse, D.: *et al* 33
Munshi, K.: and Rosenzweig, M. 4
Muslims 31–46; gendered educational choices 31–46; Jharkhand (East India) 31–46

National Health Service (NHS) hospital system 55–6
National Institute of Population Research and Training (NIPORT) 13, 18
National Rural Employment Guarantee Programme 40
National Thermal Power Corporation (NTCP) 35
National Vocational Qualifications (NVQs) 57–60
Naved, R.: Amin, S. and Newby, M. 16
Nedeva, M. 60
New Literacy Studies 80
New Modern English School 69
New Primary Schools (NPS) 37–44
Newby, M.: Naved, R. and Amin, S. 16
Ni Laoire, C. 89
Nisbett, N. 12
Nurse Midwifery Council (NMC) 53, 57
Nurse on the Move (Crowne) 49
nurses 5–6, 49–62; adaptation barriers and licences 53–4, 57–9; costly itineraries, fees and agencies 56–7; migration and role of education 52–4; mobility through migration 49–50; policy implications 59–61; Polish 52; South Asian migration to UK 5–6; study methodology 54–5; transnational flows of skilled labour 50–2; visas and work regulations/permits 54, 58–9
Nussbaum, M. 35

Occupational Travellers 109–10
Office for Standards in Education (OFSTED) 104, 107, 112
O'Hanlon, C.: and Holmes, P. 107–9
O'Hanlon, R. 5–6, 66, 103–18
Osella, F.: and Gardener, K. 1; and Osella, C. 12
oshikkito (uneducated) 16
Other Backward Castes 35–6
Ozden, C.: and Schiff, M. 4

Paci, P.: and Serneels, P. 78
Padfield, P.: and Jordan, E. 112
Pahl, K.: and Rowsell, J. 2
Palsson, G. 88
Panchamukhi, P.: and Mehrotra, S. 42
Parrenas, R. 50
Passeron, J.: and Bourdieu, P. 3, 32–4, 41–2, 105, 109
Patrinos, H.: and Psacharopoulos, G. 79
Phillips, N. 54, 60
Piketty, T. 2
Plowden Report 107
Pollner, M. 70
Popkewitz, T. 91
poradhin (depdendent) 22
Power, C. 107
Prakash, G.: and Haynes, D. 11
Pritchett, L. 79
Pryor, J. 38
Psacharopoulos, G.: and Patrinos, H. 79
Public Services International 61
purdah (curtain) 23–7

Quisumbing, A. 79

Rabinow, P. 73
Race Relations Act 108
Race Relations (Amendment) Act 110
Raghuram, P.: and Kofman, E. 51, 60
Raheja, G.: and Gold, A. 11
Rahman, R. 79
Rajaram College 69
Rao, N. 2–6, 31–47; and Jackson, C. 33
Rapoport, H.: and McKenzie, D. 4
Reed Danahay, D. 89
Ringold, D.: *et al* 111
Rivkin, S.: and Hanushek, E. 109
Robinson-Pant, A. 4, 79

INDEX

Rose, M. 88
Rose, P. 3, 34; and Dyer, C. 3, 78
Rosenzweig, M.: and Munshi, K. 4
Rowsell, J.: and Pahl, K. 2
Rozario, S. 15

Sachar, R. 35
Sahibganj College 36–7
samaj (society or moral community) 13–26
Santal tribe 35–43
Sarva Shiksha Abhiyan (SSA) 37
Save the Children 81, 104, 107–10
Scheduled Tribes (Castes) 5, 32–46, 63–74; gendered educational choices 31–46; Jharkhand (East India) 31–46
Schiff, M.: and Ozden, C. 4
Schuler, S.: *et al* 12
Secondary School Certificate (SSC) 17, 32
Seeley, J.: and Khan, I. 78, 84; Maddox, B. and Islam, M. 78, 83
Selim, N.: Kamal Waiz, N. and Amin, S. 12–16
Sen, A. 26; and Dreze, J. 3
Sen, B.: and Hulme, D. 78
Serneels, P.: and Paci, P. 78
shadhin (independent) 22–3
shadinota (independence) 20
Sharoff, L.: and Yorks, L. 52
shekna (mature) 17
shikkito (educated) 16
Siddiqui, T. 2; and Abrar, C. 4
Skeldon, R. 2
skill transfers and brain drain 3–4
Smyth, J.: and Hattam, R. 88
social mobility and status 63–76; and anthropology 70–4; educational achievements 69–70; Kolhapur 63–74; life histories 63–74; the Pundat family 67–70; strategies and contingencies 66–7; untouchable communities 63–74; versus kin and caste ties 68–9
songsar (nuclear family) 13
Soros, G. 110
Stead, J.: and Lloyd, G. 104
Sterland, L.: and Talbott-Strettle, L. 52
Stockdale, A. 89
Strauss, A.: and Corbin, J. 55
Street, B. 80
Stromquist, N. 12, 60
Subrahmanian, R. 12
Swann Report 107

Tagore College 14–27; Intermediate exam passes and failures 20–1; occupation and marital status of pupils *20*
Tala 14–27
Talbott-Strettle, L.: and Sterland, L. 52

Tarapur 14–27
Theobald, P. 90
Thieme, S.: and Wyss, S. 1
Thompson, P. 68; and Bertaux, D. 2, 4, 63–6, 70
Thorlindsson, T.: and Bjarnason, T. 89
Thorne, S. 52
Thorsen, D. 2
Traveller Education Support Service 107, 114
Trostel, M. 79
Tumin, M. 64

UK Border Agency 58, 61
United Nations Children's Fund (UNICF) 12, 104, 111
United Nations Educational, Scientific and Cultural Organisation (UNESCO) 12–13, 18
Unnithan-Kumar, M. 33
untouchable communities 5–6, 63–76; dialogic construction 73–4; naming and erasure 71–3
Ureta, M.: and Edwards, A. 1
Urry, J. 55
Usher, R. 87, 90

Visaria, L. 12

Walby, S. 60–1
Walters, S. 50
Warrington, C. 104, 110
Weber, Max 34
Wenger, E. 88
Where I Belong study 89–90
Whitehead, A. 26
Wiborg, A. 89
Wilkin, A.: Derrington, C. and Foster, B. 114
Williams, R. 25–6
Willis, P. 33, 105
Winkleman-Gleed, A. 51
Wolf, E. 67
Wood, G. 78
World Bank 12
World Conference on Women, Beijing (1995) 61
Wright Mills, C. 73
Wyss, S.: and Thieme, S. 1

Yang, D. 1
Yeates, N. 50
Yorks, L.: and Sharoff, L. 52
Young, I. 2
youth aspirations 6, 87–101; Atlantic Canadian rural community 87–101; brain drain 91–9; timing and pressure 94–6

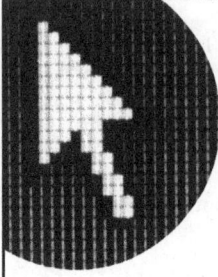

Taylor & Francis Author Services

publish with us

The **Taylor & Francis Author Services** department aims to enhance your publishing experience as a journal author and optimize the impact of your article in the global research community. Assistance and support is available – from preparing the submission of your article through to setting up citation alerts post-publication on Informaworld.

Our **Author Services** department can provide advice on how to:

- Direct your submission to the correct journal
- Prepare your manuscript according to the journal's requirements
- Maximize your article's citations
- Submit supplementary data for online publication
- Submit your article online via ScholarOne Manuscripts
- Apply for permission to reproduce images
- Prepare your illustrations for print
- Track the status of your manuscript through the production process
- Return your corrections online
- Purchase reprints through *Rightslink*
- Register for article citation alerts
- Take advantage of our *iOpenAccess* option
- Access your article online
- Benefit from rapid online publication via *iFirst*

For further information go to:
www.tandf.co.uk/journals/authorservices

Or contact:

Author Services Manager, Taylor & Francis Group,
4 Park Square, Milton Park, Abingdon, Oxon OX14 4RN UK
Email: **authorqueries@tandf.co.uk**

www.routledge.com/9780415672276

Related titles from Routledge

The Internationalisation of Higher Education
Towards a new research agenda in critical higher education studies
Edited by Eva Hartmann

We are in the middle of a fundamental transformation of the global architecture which is challenging the supremacy of the US, and to a certain extent of Europe, in economic and also in normative terms. The essays in this volume shed light on the role of higher education (HE) and its internationalisation in this transformation, focusing on the different regions of the world. These empirical studies are part of a new research agenda in HE studies, going beyond a 'higher educationism' limiting itself to a simple description of institutional changes in HE in the light of internationalisation. They advance an interdisciplinary perspective drawing on accounts from critical theory, international relations and international political economy. This perspective analyses the strategic selectivity, transformation and struggles related to this major transformation of HE and its contribution to a new global architecture.

This book was originally published as a special issue of *Globalisation, Societies and Education*.

> June 2011: 246 x 174: 160pp
> Hb: 978-0-415-67227-6
> £80 / $125

For more information and to order a copy visit
www.routledge.com/9780415672276

Available from all good bookshops

www.routledge.com/9780415673020

Related titles from Routledge

The Education of Black Males in a 'Post-Racial' World

Edited by Anthony L. Brown & Jamel K. Donnor

The Education of Black Males in a 'Post-Racial' World examines the varied structural and discursive contexts of race, masculinities and class that shape the educational and social lives of Black males. The contributing authors take direct aim at the current discourses that construct Black males as disengaged in schooling because of an autonomous Black male culture, and explore how media, social sciences, school curriculum, popular culture and sport can define and constrain the lives of Black males. The chapters also provide alternative methodologies, theories and analyses for making sense of and addressing the complex needs of Black males in schools and in society. By expanding our understanding of how unequal access to productive opportunities and quality resources converge to systemically create disparate experiences and outcomes for African-American males, this volume powerfully illustrates that race *still* matters in 'post-racial' America.

This book was originally published as a special issue of the journal *Race Ethnicity and Education*.

August 2011: 246 x 174: 152pp
Hb: 978-0-415-67302-0
£80 / $125

For more information and to order a copy visit
www.routledge.com/9780415673020

Available from all good bookshops

www.routledge.com/9780415693523

Related titles from Routledge

Education and Religion
Global Pressures, Local Responses
Edited by Keith Watson & William I. Ozanne

In most countries, secular or otherwise, education and religion are closely interlinked; no matter how hard the state tries, it can be difficult to remove the ties between them. This book investigates the links between education, religion and politics.

The dominant feature in creating a common culture between peoples, each of which has its own distinct heritage and practices, is religion. Globalisation is leading to a redefinition of the state, community and local identity. Recent world events have focused attention on the interplay between education, religion and politics like never before. Even more pertinent is the fact that the involvement of politics in decisions about religion and education is often central and impossible to disentangle.

Education and Religion covers all the major religious traditions – Buddhist, Christian, Jewish, Hindu, Muslim, Sikh – and cites global examples throughout the world. It aims to understand the underlying complexities in the struggle to reconcile education, religion and politics in an informative and sensitive way.

This book was originally published as a special issue of *Comparative Education*.

December 2011: 246 x 174: 160pp
Hb: 978-0-415-69352-3
£80 / $125

For more information and to order a copy visit
www.routledge.com/9780415693523

Available from all good bookshops

www.routledge.com/9780415693493

Related titles from Routledge

Education and Global Justice

Edited by Michele Schweisfurth & Clive Harber

Education and Global Justice discusses key themes concerning the relationship between education and global justice in a varied series of highly relevant national contexts. Major international issues such as war, conflict and peace, social justice and injustice, multicultural education, inclusion, privatisation and democracy are explored in relation to the Middle East, Colombia, South Korea, India, Uganda and Pakistan. An interdisciplinary approach is also taken to explore both the nature of global justice and the possibilities for education for global justice in the future. Some of the contents of the book may surprise or even shock readers who like to think that education is inherently and solely a force for good in an unjust world. Instead, in discussing the realities, resistances and challenges facing education for global justice, the contributors show that education can be harmful to individuals and societies while maintaining a hopeful view of education's potential to contribute to greater global social justice.

This book was originally published as a special issue of the journal *Educational Review*.

January 2012: 246 x 174: 116pp
Hb: 978-0-415-69349-3
£80 / $125

For more information and to order a copy visit
www.routledge.com/9780415693493

Available from all good bookshops

Compare:
A Journal of Comparative and International Education

The official journal of the British Association for International and Comparative Education (BAICE)

Edited by **Paul Morris**, *Institute of Education, University of London, UK*, **Nitya Rao**, *University of East Anglia, UK* and **Yusuf Sayed**, *University of Sussex, UK*

Comparative and international studies in education enjoy new popularity. They illuminate the effects of globalisation and post-structural thinking on learning for professional and personal lives. **Compare** publishes such research as it relates to educational development and change in different parts of the world. It seeks analyses of educational discourse, policy and practice across disciplines, and their implications for teaching, learning and management.

The editors welcome papers which reflect on practice from early childhood to the end of adult life, review processes of comparative and international enquiry and report on empirical studies. All papers should include a comparative dimension. Case studies of under-researched aspects of the field and countries about which little is known are of particular interest.

Get more from Routledge Education Journals!

You can now find special offers, exclusive articles and audio interviews online:

Education Arena
Taylor & Francis Group
Visit the Education Arena journal website. Connecting you to global education research:
www.educationarena.com

twitter
Follow us on twitter:
www.twitter.com/educationarena

facebook
Become a fan on Facebook:
www.facebook.com/educationarena

www.tandfonline.com/compare